S. SHAKTHIDHARAN is a western Sydney storyteller with Sri Lankan heritage and Tamil ancestry. He's a writer, director and producer of theatre and film, and composer of original music. His debut play *Counting and Cracking* (Belvoir and Co-Curious, Associate Writer Eamon Flack), received critical, commercial and community acclaim at the 2019 Sydney and Adelaide Festivals. Shakthi was also a Producer and Associate Director on the work. The script won the Victorian Premier's Literature Prize and the NSW Premier's Nick Enright Prize for Playwriting; the production won seven Helpmann and three Sydney Theatre Awards. It toured in 2022 to Edinburgh Festival and Birmingham Rep to similar acclaim. Shakthi's most recent play *The Jungle and the Sea* with Belvoir (co-written and directed with Eamon Flack), again met with rave reviews and had a profound impact on the Sri Lankan community. It won four Sydney Theatre Awards in January 2023 including Best Mainstage Production. Shakthi wrote and directed 宿*(stay)* for Sydney Festival 2022; wrote an adaptation of Zana Fraillon's *The Bone Sparrow* which toured the UK with Pilot Theatre; and has in development his first novel, a new play with Belvoir, a feature film with Felix Media and a new TV project. He's the Director of Kurinji and previous to this was Founder/Artistic Lead of Co-Curious (2018-2022), sister company to CuriousWorks where he was Founder and Artistic Director (2003-2018). Shakthi was the Carriageworks inaugural Associate Artist and is a recipient of both the Phillip Parson's and Kirk Robson awards.

EAMON FLACK is the Artistic Director of Belvoir St Theatre in Sydney. He is a director, writer, dramaturg and script developer. He was born in Singapore and grew up in Singapore, Darwin, Cootamundra and Brisbane. He graduated from the acting course at WAAPA and has since worked around Australia and internationally, from the Tiwi Islands to Sri Lanka and the UK. He has led Belvoir's new work development in various guises since 2006. His directing credits include acclaimed productions of *Angels in America*, *The Glass Menagerie* and *Counting and Cracking* (with Associate Director S. Shakthidharan) and the premiers of Rita Kalnejais's *Babyteeth* and Tommy Murphy's *Holding the Man*. His adaptations include Gorky's *Summerfolk*, Ibsen's *Ghosts*, Sophocles's *Antigone*, and Chekhov's *Ivanov* and *The Cherry Orchard*. He was Associate Writer on S. Shakthidharan's *Counting and Cracking*, winner of the Nick Enright Prize for Playwriting at the NSW Premier's Literary Awards, the Victorian Literary Prize and the Victorian Premier's Award for Drama. His work has won multiple Helpmann Awards and Sydney Theatre Awards.

THE JUNGLE
AND THE SEA

காடும் கடலும்

ගණ වන මුහුද

S. SHAKTHIDHARAN
AND EAMON FLACK

CURRENCY PRESS
The performing arts publisher

CURRENCY PLAYS

First published in 2023
by Currency Press Pty Ltd,
Gadigal Land, Suite 310, 46–56 Kippax Street, Surry Hills, NSW 2010, Australia
enquiries@currency.com.au
www.currency.com.au
Typeset by Lucinda Naughton for Currency Press.
Cover design by Lisa White for Currency Press.

Currency Press acknowledges the Traditional Owners of the Country on which
we live and work. We pay our respects to all Aboriginal and Torres Straight
Islander Elders, past and present.

A catalogue record for this
book is available from the
NATIONAL LIBRARY
OF AUSTRALIA   National Library of Australia

Contents

Introduction   *vii*
   Abarna Raj

Creators' notes   *xiii*

THE JUNGLE AND THE SEA

Act One   1

Act Two   21

Act Three   30

Act Four   59

Act Five   74

Kalieaswari Srinivasan, Anandavalli, Nadie Kammallaweera, Prakash Belawadi, Emma Harvie and Biman Wimalaratne in Belvoir St Theatre's The Jungle and the Sea, *2022 (Photo: Sriram Jeyaraman)*

Introduction

Across the extended period of the Sri Lankan Civil War (1983–2009), there arose brief instances when fear momentarily recedes, granting passage for laughter to break through. In *The Jungle and the Sea's* initial scene, we are introduced to Lakshmi, Ahilan, Abi, and Madhu. These fleeting moments detach us momentarily from the backdrop of their lives, immersing us in their immediate world—a world adorned with playful banter, budding romance, and easy-going conversations. Yet, this veneer of normality is shattered abruptly by an unforeseen air raid, which tragically claims the lives of mothers and children. This sudden shift mirrors the unpredictable nature of prolonged conflict. Just as we partake in their laughter, we are swiftly thrust into the same stark reality they confront—where laughter can so quickly give way to fear.

Amidst the panic that ensues, families scramble frantically for safety. Siva, the father of Abi, Madhu, Ahilan and Lakshmi, steps forward to guide people toward the local church, believing it to be a sanctuary. However, as the church transforms into a target, Siva stands in stunned silence. The weight of realisation descends upon him—the church he guided families to has been devastated by a bomb, and he was the one who directed them there for safety.

The Sri Lankan Civil War resulted in the deaths of hundreds of thousands and displayed a blatant disregard for humanitarian law and the rules of warfare. By deliberately targeting religious and civilian structures, the conflict not only propagated violence but also shattered the sense of security for civilians caught in its midst.

Amidst the chaos following the air raids, Ahilan, Siva's son, crosses paths with a commander from the Liberation Tigers of Tamil Eelam (LTTE), the revolutionary movement leading the war efforts against the Sri Lankan Government. The LTTE's cause revolves around securing the rights of the Tamil minority and establishing a recognised homeland called 'Eelam', believing it to be the sole solution to end generations of violations against the minority Tamil communities.

In a conflict of this nature, those at the forefront must grapple with their personal ideologies to decide how they will fight for justice. Influenced by his compassionate father Siva, Ahilan staunchly believes in the triumph of truth through evidence and peace. Conversely, the LTTE commander advocates for a different approach—seizing power through strength. In their ensuing dialogue, the LTTE commander highlights the implausibility of truth prevailing, as it would necessitate a shared humanity that has eroded over time. Ultimately, Ahilan is swayed by this perspective.

When Ahilan's mother, Gowrie and sister, Abi learn of Ahilan's decision to join the LTTE through the commander, they refuse to accept this truth. They believe that he could have only arrived at such a choice due to the manipulation of his boyish naivety and kindness. Gowrie is overcome by a sense of guilt for not being by her son's side when he encountered the LTTE commander. She acknowledges that she failed to shield Ahilan, who was a boy seeking to transition into manhood and step up amidst the tragedies that were unfolding around him. In a poignant display of emotion, Gowrie tears at her sari and covers her eyes, symbolising her commitment to find her son and be together with all four of her children.

Gowrie's act of blindfolding might seem unfamiliar from a Western perspective, yet it holds profound significance within the depths of Hindu traditions. Embedded within this cultural core is the act of embracing suffering—the suffering stemming from one's own mistakes and the ensuing pain they have caused, serving as an enduring reminder of the singular purpose now guiding Gowrie's life—to correct the mistake, in this instance, to find Ahilan.

As the war escalates, the family confronts a heart-wrenching decision—they cannot leave Ahilan behind and so they take a risk and temporarily separate, hopeful for a reunion. Lakshmi and her father Siva go to Australia for safety, while Gowrie and her daughters Abi and Madhu continue their quest to find Ahilan.

As the play progresses, we follow Abi's struggle. She shoulders the responsibility of finding Ahilan while guiding her blindfolded mother through the challenges of the battlefield and the aftermath of the Sri Lankan Civil War. This journey showcases the potency of tradition, the weight of sacrifice, and the deep love propelling their unwavering determination.

In the second act of the play, we step into the new lives of Siva and his daughter Lakshmi as they embark on the journey of rebuilding in Australia. This new phase brings various opportunities for Lakshmi, like pursuing a career in law, having the opportunity to attend upscale restaurants, and freely exploring her own sexual identity. Amid these transformations, we witness Siva's guilt stemming from his role in a tragic church bombing that claimed multiple lives.

Lakshmi also grapples with inner turmoil. She stands torn between her evolving Australian identity and the heavy guilt of being the one who managed to escape. This struggle becomes starkly evident in the closing scenes when her sister Abi tells her, 'You go. Back to where you are from,' implying their paths have diverged so much that Lakshmi no longer belongs to her homeland but to Australia.

The play's intensity peaks as it delves into the climactic moment, the final battle of the Sri Lankan Civil War (May 2009). This heart-wrenching account unfolds through the firsthand experiences of Abi, Madhu and Gowrie, as well as the poignant dialogues between Lakshmi and her father Siva.

In this harrowing phase of the war, violence surged to horrifying heights, leaving behind a landscape of shattered human rights and indescribable anguish. Surrender, symbolised by the white flag, was met with disdain. Hospitals, once refuges for the wounded and helpless, were mercilessly attacked, resulting in unimaginable devastation. Amidst this chaos, thousands from the LTTE were taken hostage, only to vanish into thin air, igniting an international outcry that would lead to a UN investigation.

The principles of warfare were callously discarded, guided by a resolute president's determination not only to conclude the war but to obliterate any remnants of hope for future uprisings. In this stark portrayal, the play unflinchingly exposes the ruthless course that history took, revealing the raw brutality that can emerge when the rules of humanity are cast aside.

In the play, we witness Lakshmi's rising anger as she listens from Australia to the unfolding events in her homeland through the radio. This sentiment is shared by many in the diaspora community. Many of the Sri Lankan Tamil diaspora had family or loved ones entangled in the war and relied on news reports to comprehend the situation, often different from what they heard from those on the ground. What echoed across the Tamil diaspora was a strong conviction that the LTTE wouldn't easily surrender.

Over the span of 30 years, hundreds of thousands of people sought refuge from the war in safer countries such as Australia and Switzerland. Throughout the war, they played a vital role from advocacy, economic support and the rebuilding agenda. Amidst periods of intense fighting and brief moments of peace, the LTTE managed to maintain a surprising balance of power despite their limited resources and the use of controversial tactics.

However, the events of May 2009, particularly the final battle, caught everyone off guard.

The devastating impact of the 2004 Boxing Day tsunami on military infrastructure and human resources five years earlier, internal conflicts within the LTTE's leadership, and China's growing political influence in the conflict all contributed to favouring the Sri Lankan Government. President Rajapaksa's unwavering determination to end the war, coupled with a nationalistic stance, further influenced this shift.

The last weeks and days of the conflict left everyone in shock. The ending was brutal, just as the president had foretold. It resulted in a mix of shattered hopes and triumphant cheers, depending on which side of the conflict one stood.

In the play, Lakshmi's brave decision to return to the heart of the conflict in order to bring her family back home becomes a focal point. Her father's deep concern was palpable, fully aware of the slim chances of a safe return.

Lakshmi successfully reaches the conflict zone and reunites with her mother Gowrie and sister Abi. However, she also learns of her brother's death. Amidst a heated exchange between Abi and government officials, Lakshmi implores her sister to accompany her back to Australia.

In the poignant conversation between Abi and Lakshmi, two individuals who once shared a common starting point now find themselves on divergent paths, shaped by the challenges they faced. Abi, despite enduring injustice, has cultivated resilience, empowering her to champion justice. Conversely, Lakshmi recognises the futility of such efforts and the inherent risks linked to standing up for the truth.

This crossroad of belief brings forth a profound moral quandary:

should we unwaveringly adhere to our truths, even as the world crumbles around us, or should we weigh the costs and benefits before unveiling the truth? Lakshmi, having gained insights into the true costs and experienced a glimpse of a better life in Australia, finds herself liberated from the urgency of immediate truth revelation. Conversely, for Abi, the imperative is to uphold the truth, regardless of the incurred costs. In this intricate tapestry of choices and convictions, we are confronted with the complexities of human essence—the interplay between steadfast ideals and the pragmatic dance of life's intricate threads.

We see that ultimately everyone has a different truth. For Abi it had become the honouring of her brother with his burial rights, as a proper burial is seen as a way to ensure that the soul transitions peacefully and is not hindered in its journey by unresolved matters associated with the body. For Lakshmi it is about justice in a framework where there is a

Rajan Velu, Kalieaswari Srinivasan, Anandavalli, Nadie Kammallaweera and Jacob Rajan in Belvoir St Theatre's The Jungle and the Sea, *2022 (Photo: Sriram Jeyaraman)*

greater chance of resolve—gathering evidence on the human right abuses, and for Gowrie—the truth is about life itself. That this life is presented to us—in all its pain and all its glory—for the ultimate redemption of humanity.

In the final scene, even though Gowrie can't physically hold her son's hand, a symbolic reunion unfolds and her blindfold can finally be lifted. In this poignant moment, this act signifies not only a closure but also a profound revelation—the revelation that in embracing their distinct truths, they each contribute to the larger truth of life's intricate journey, marked by struggles and triumphs, leading toward the ultimate redemption of humanity.

This play peels away the layers of war's horror to unveil the personal stories concealed beneath the echoing bombs, the haunting traces of devastation, and the sombre media reports chronicling obliterated lives. The Sri Lankan Civil War, with all its agony and heartache, demands to be recounted. Without history's preservation and sharing of narratives, the tale of human suffering and resilience risks fading away.

In a land where echoes of nationalistic ambitions persist, this play becomes a beacon of hope. It stands as evidence of the power of documentation, a call for both present and future generations. It serves as an indelible reminder: knowledge propels us forward, offering the means to rectify past injustices and to ascend upon the accumulated wisdom of preceding eras. Through learning from their missteps, we can ensure that we never let history repeat itself.

Abarna Raj

Abarna Raj is the Founding Director of Palmera, a for purpose organisation that works to economically empower vulnerable families in Sri Lanka. You can read more about Palmera's projects and make a donation at www.palmera.org.

Creators' Notes

During war, life goes on. Even amidst violence and degradation there is still love, determination, cheekiness and delight. *Counting and Cracking* was written in honour of those who tried to halt Sri Lanka's descent into civil war. *The Jungle and the Sea* is written in honour of those who lived through the war, and the ways they found to uphold their dignity even when everything else was falling down around them. I am eternally grateful to the many, many Sri Lankans who shared their deepest truths and fears with me in the process of writing this work.

After war, a nation is at a crossroads. How its leaders decide to tell the story of that war will shape the country's future for decades to come. Thirteen years since the civil war ended in Sri Lanka, there is still so much unresolved; so much unfinished business. A nation cannot heal in this state.

Sri Lanka is at a crossroads again today. I hope this play can be one small part of a process which helps my community turn an open heart to its past; and resolve to not repeat those mistakes in our future.

The *Mahabharata* and *Antigone* radically opened up the process of writing *The Jungle and the Sea*. These ancient texts gave us permission to depict the lives of ordinary people as that of something extraordinary —almost mythic. The result, somehow, is something even more true, even more real. The final work is fiercely its own thing, but we are indebted to these texts for the potential they were able to unleash in its form.

It took ten years to research and write *Counting and Cracking*. Six years to convince the wider industry it was a story worth telling on the mainstage. Four years to cast that incredible ensemble of actors. Compared to all that, *The Jungle and Sea* feels like it has happened in a flash. That a Sri Lankan story, with an international ensemble, might be part of the new normal here in the Australian arts industry does feel like genuine change. It needs to be a change that will continue.

S. Shakthidharan

Emma Harvie, Prakash Belawadi, Nadie Kammallaweera and Anandavalli in Belvoir St Theatre's The Jungle and the Sea, *2022 (Photo: Sriram Jeyaraman)*

In her essay 'The Iliad, or Poem of Force', the philosopher Simone Weil writes about the 'force' unleashed by war: 'From its first property (the ability to turn a human being into a thing by the simple method of killing him) flows another, quite prodigious too in its own way, the ability to turn a human being into a thing while he is still alive.'

This is a play about people who refuse to become things while they are still alive.

Even when war has turned life into chaos, these characters go on finding ways to make their own choices any which way they can. The actions they take are inspired by real stories of real people in Sri Lanka, and by characters from three great works of ancient literature—the *Mahabharatha*, and Sophocles' *Antigone* and *Oedipus at Colonus*. From these works we've plucked particular moments and used them like seeds to grow our own storylines and characters, with the exception of Act Four which is very much a version of *Antigone*. The seeds we picked are all moments of human choice made in the face of chaos: a promise, a curse, a marriage, an act of reverence for the dead …

Our characters are fictional, but the events that intervene in their imaginary lives are real events which took place in the north of Sri Lanka in recent decades. The facts and details that make up the circumstances of the play are drawn from the mass of uncollected testimony that forms the history of the Sri Lankan Civil War, and the situations faced by the characters were a reality for hundreds of thousands of people.

The play is written to be performed with a revolve and you couldn't do the play without it. Most obviously it allows us to stage a small model of the terrible forced exodus which took place in the Vanni in 2009. But it does much more than make walking scenes possible. From workshopping an earlier project we'd begun to see ways that a revolve can support a kind of swift image-making storytelling in a way that a fixed stage can't. A turning stage can move easily between the epic and intimate, it can evoke landscape and time in ways a fixed stage can't, it can move the action through time, it can contain multiple situations, it has a heightened ability for costumes and props to suggest a bigger picture, all while keeping the focus of the stage on the people. The revolve in this play is more than a useful staging tool, it is a kind of

force of history, fate, memory at work on the characters.
This play was conceived from the outset as a collaboration with
Lingalyam Dance Company, founded and led by Anandavalli. Lingalyam
is one of the country's great independent arts companies, and its proud
history of using traditional artforms in new ways to tell stories about
the contemporary world is an inspiration. There is a lot that is new and
bewildering about the twenty-first century, but more and more I find
myself thinking that there are some human experiences that you can only
get a grip on through the wisdom and rigour of old forms. I certainly
thought that any time I saw Ananadavalli dance at the beginning and
the end of the show.

Many of these characters were written specially for the actors who
originated them. That original company was a heroic team of artists and
crew, full of joy and love and rigour. Their contribution to this show
goes far deeper than is normal.

நாங்கள் மறக்கவே மாட்டோம்.
'We will never forget.'
Gowrie, Act Three.

Eamon Flack

The Jungle and the Sea was first produced by Belvoir St Theatre, Gadigal country, Sydney, on 12 November, 2022, with the following cast:

GOWRIE	Anandavalli
ABI	Kalieaswari Srinivasan
SIVA, FR JAMES & OTHERS	Prakash Belawadi
LAKSHMI & OTHERS	Emma Harvie
MADHU & OTHERS	Nadie Kammallaweera
KISHAN & OTHERS	Jacob Rajan
HIMAL & OTHERS	Rajan Velu
AHILAN & OTHERS	Biman Wimalaratne
MUSICIAN (VEENA)	Indu Balachandran
MUSICIAN (MRIDANGAM & VOCALS)	Arjunan Puveendran
COVER	Kaivalya Suvarna

Writers & Directors, S. Shakthidharan and Eamon Flack
Choreographer & Cultural Advisor, Anandavalli
Set & Costume Designer, Dale Ferguson
Lighting Designer, Veronique Benett
Composer, Arjunan Puveendran
Sound Designer, Steve Francis
Musical Supervisor, Alan John
Fight Director, Tim Dashwood
Fight Director, Nigel Poulton
Vocal & Accent Coach, Laura Farrell
Vocal Coach, Amy Hume
Design Associate, Keerthi Subramanyam
Assistant Director, Nithya Nagarajan
Community Engagement Coordinator, Sujan Selven
Audience Development Coordinator, Thinesh Thillai
Stage Manager, Luke McGettigan
Deputy Stage Manager, Ayah Tayeh
Assistant Stage Manager, Nitya Ganesh
Assistant Stage Manager, Tom Rogers

CHARACTERS

GOWRIE, (amma) Sri Lankan Tamil, Hindu, female, mother of ABI, MADHU, AHILAN and LAKSHMI

SIVA, (Sivapalan, appa) Sri Lankan Tamil, Christian, male, father of ABI, MADHU, AHILAN and LAKSHMI

ABI, (Abirami, akka) Sri Lankan Tamil, Hindu, female

MADHU, (akka) Sri Lankan Tamil, Christian, female

AHILAN, (thumbi) Sri Lankan Tamil, Hindu, male

LAKSHMI, (thangachi) Sri Lankan Tamil, Hindu, female

KISHAN, (thatha) Singhalese, Christian, male, father to HIMAL

HIMAL, (putha) Singhalese, Buddhist, male

SALIM, Sri Lankan Tamil, (Sufi) Muslim, male

WOMAN ONE, Salim's wife, Sri Lankan Tami, (Sufi) Muslim, female

SURGEON, Sri Lankan Tamil, male

COMMANDER, Sri Lankan Tamil, male

FATHER JAMES, Sri Lankan Tamil, Catholic priest, male

UN WORKER, Sri Lankan Tamil, male

WOMAN TWO, on a bicycle, Sri Lankan Tamil, female

FARMER, Sri Lankan Tamil, male

DOCTOR, Sri Lankan Tamil, male

TRO WOMAN, Sri Lankan Tamil

LTTE RECRUITER, Sri Lankan Tamil, male

AGA MAN ONE, Sri Lankan Tamil

AGA MAN TWO, Sri Lankan Tamil

RED CROSS WORKER, Sri Lankan Tamil

LTTE SOLDIER, Sri Lankan Tamil, male

SOLDIER ONE, Sri Lankan Army soldier, Singhalese, male

SEWING WOMAN, Sri Lankan Tamil

SOLDIER TWO, Sri Lankan Army soldier, Singhalese, male

DEVLA-MA, Sri Lankan, Vedda, female

DOUBLING SUGGESTIONS

Siva / Father James / Farmer

Abi / Woman one

Madhu / Devla-Ma

Lakshmi / Woman two / TRO woman / Sewing woman

Ahilan / LTTE Recruiter / Soldier one

Kishan / Surgeon / Commander / UN worker / Doctor / AGA man

Himal / Salim / Soldier two / Red Cross worker

SETTING

The play takes place between 1995 and 2022.

Act One—Jaffna and Navali, Sri Lanka

Act Two—Bennelong Point and Guildford, Sydney

Acts Three and Four—The Vanni, Sri Lanka

Act Five—Guildford, Sydney; Nanthikkadal Lagoon, Sri Lanka

KEY TAMIL WORDS

amma—mother

appa—father

anna—older brother

akka—older sister

thangaci—younger sister

thumbi—younger brother

mahan—son

KEY SINHALA WORDS

thatha—father

putha—son

NOTES

The dance in this play is called Bharathanatyam. It's a classical Indian art form still practiced widely today. Its ancestral home is Tamil Nadu in the south of India, but it's also part of the fabric of life for the Tamil people in the north of Sri Lanka (these groups also share the same language). Bharathanatyam is a vibrant, emotive dance form made up of two primary movement types: 'jathis' or passages of complex, energetic footwork and rhythm; and 'abhinaya' or passages of highly emotional and suggestive mime, focusing around the face and hands.

The play is written to take place on a revolve. It starts turning as noted at the top of the play and continues turning until the end. When scenes are in a single location it turns slowly but does not stop. In the walking scenes it turns at various walking speeds as required.

The play is an original work drawing on three different sources: a diverse and large collection of personal testimony about the Sri Lankan Civil War, particularly its final stages; certain narrative and symbolic strands from the *Mahabharatha*, in particular the Ghandhara story; the Thebes cycles of Sophocles and Aeschylus. Act Four is loosely based on Sophocles' *Antigone*.

There are intervals after Act Two and Act Three.

No violence is shown on stage. The deaths are stylised.

PROLOGUE

Jaffna, Sri Lanka, 2022.

GOWRIE *(60s) is blindfolded and dances.*

After some time, KISHAN *enters.*

He watches for a moment, then speaks.

KISHAN: Gowrie-Amma.
GOWRIE: Kishan?
KISHAN: Gowrie-Amma. They have found the bodies.

ACT ONE

Navali, Sri Lanka, 1995.

ABI, MADHU, AHILAN *and* LAKSHMI, *all teenagers, are walking to the beach. They are carrying study books, beach towels, cricket gear and snacks.* ABI *uses a puffer occasionally.*

ABI: Evolution occurs through a process that involves what events?
MADHU: One, Variation. Two, Changes to the gene pool. Three, Struggle for existence. / Four, Reproduction. Five, Survival of the fittest.
ABI: Chi chi chi.
AHILAN: Blergh. It's so hot.
ABI: Right events, wrong order / I think.
AHILAN: Lakshmi, you bat.
LAKSHMI: I have to practice!
ABI: Variation, gene pool and reproduction / first.
AHILAN: Dance class is finished now!
LAKSHMI: Amma told me to practice.
AHILAN: Aaaaarrrggggghhhh.
MADHU: [*to* ABI] Thank god we were bad dancers.

> *The sisters laugh.*

ABI: When's your exam?
MADHU: Tuesday. Three pm. In the Ladies College. You?

AHILAN: [*to* ABI *and* MADHU] You're so boring!
ABI: Thursday. Nine am.
MADHU: In the morning, that's better. I get sleepy in the afternoon.

> AHILAN *gives* MADHU *the cricket bat.*

AHILAN: Madhu-Akka, go bat.
MADHU: I'm studying!
AHILAN: So?

> MADHU *continues walking and reciting the cycle of evolution, in Tamil and in English, as she holds the bat.*

Abi-Akka, you're fielding, you're silly point okay—
ABI: Silly what?
AHILAN: Just field, okay?
ABI: I'm always fielding!
AHILAN: Well you can't bowl—
MADHU: And you can't bat—

> *They crack up.*

ABI: Idiots.

> AHILAN *starts stretching.*

MADHU: What are you doing thumbi?
AHILAN: Getting ready to demolish you!
MADHU: [*laughing*] But you're an off-spinner!
AHILAN: [*commentating*] And Muralitharan is coming in to bowl. What will he bowl this time, a googly? A watermelon?
MADHU: [*laughing*] Stop distracting me thumbi!

> AHILAN *bowls.* MADHU *plays a magnificent shot—*

LAKSHMI: Six! A six!
ABI: Where did the ball go?

> *Except someone catches it—*HIMAL.

MADHU: Himal no!
AHILAN: Yes! / Yes yes yes yes yes! Caught out.
HIMAL: [*in Sinhala and Tamil*] Thank you very much—
LAKSHMI: Himal! Eh Abi Himal is here!
MADHU: No it doesn't count, / it doesn't count—
AHILAN: Madhu is out for a duck.

MADHU: It doesn't count, he wasn't playing, he's just a passer-by—

AHILAN: Caught in the outfield by Himal Passer-by—

MADHU: [*calling out to* HIMAL] What are you doing, don't interfere in play!

HIMAL: Sorry but if a ball is in the air it must be caught, it is a law of life.

AHILAN: Nice catch man!

MADHU: What are you even doing here huh? Don't you know we are studying? Akka!

HIMAL: I was just passing by—

AHILAN: Himal Passer-by, always passing by.

LAKSHMI: Are you lost again, Himal Passer-by?

> *They crack up.*

AHILAN: What a *coincidence* you were just passing by on a *hot* day in the *middle of the day* when the *same-time-every-week* walk to the beach is likely to happen, *eeeeevery* Sunday, passing by—

ABI: Leave him alone.

HIMAL: Maybe I might have a little present to deliver—

AHILAN: For Abi-Akka? How convenient—

HIMAL: For Madhu.

> *He pulls a book out of his bag.*

MADHU: For me?!

ABI: For my sister?

MADHU: *Helm's Field Guide to the / Birds of Sri Lanka.*

HIMAL: [*in chorus*] Birds of Sri Lanka. It's your birthday tomorrow, no?

MADHU: Oh my god! Thank you!

> *She starts reading it immediately.*

ABI: That was very thoughtful of you.

HIMAL: [*to* ABI] And I—you see I was walking past some nice camellias—

> *He gives them to* ABI.

ABI: Did you steal these from / Selvi Aunty's?

HIMAL: Selvi Aunty has the best camellias in Jaffna—

AHILAN: Aaah don't say that to Amma okay? Patas!

LAKSHMI: Himal! Hey Passer-by! Here, look, watch!

> LAKSHMI *does part of a Bharathanatyam jathi sequence. At the end she adds a hip-hop move. They all cheer.*

GOWRIE: [*offstage*] Lakshmi! I saw that!

LAKSHMI: [*calling back*] Class is finished! Different dancing now!

GOWRIE: [*offstage*] Who is that? / Is that Himal?! What's he doing here?

KIDS: *Uh-oh!*

AHILAN: He was just passing by Amma—

MADHU: [*in Tamil and English*] Go go go—

ABI: Meet us at Casuarina beach. Go go go! / Take the flowers.

MADHU: She's coming!

LAKSHMI: Hurry / go!

> HIMAL *runs out, then comes back for the flowers—*

ABI: Go go go!

> *—Then runs out again, leaving without them.*

> LAKSHMI *waves to him while she dances the Bharathanatyam /
> hip-hop move—*

LAKSHMI: Eh, bye bye Passer-by!

> *—And doesn't notice* GOWRIE *(40s) catching up to them all until
> she is struck on the back of the head.*

GOWRIE: Idiot, what is this rubbish? If you are going to practice, practice
properly!

LAKSHMI: Yes Amma.

> *The others laugh and* GOWRIE *hits the closest—doesn't matter
> who it is.*

GOWRIE: Why was Himal here?

ABI *and* MADHU: He was just passing by Amma!

GOWRIE: You should be studying!

ABI *and* MADHU: Amma, we know it all. We know everything.

> *They rattle off the immune system and the stages of evolution to
> bad renditions of Bharathanatyam—*

GOWRIE: Stop it, I can't bear to even look at you two. I'm ashamed of
how bad you are, my own daughters.

LAKSHMI: Amma I don't like dancing either.

GOWRIE: But you are good at it, so you must do it, no? Again!

GOWRIE *recites some nattuvangam (rhythmic syllables) as* LAKSHMI
does the dance movement again.

SIVA *(40s) enters.*

AHILAN: Appa!

MADHU: What took you so long?

SIVA: [*to* GOWRIE] Father asked to meet after this morning's service. The
parish wants to build a shelter for displaced communities on our land.

GOWRIE *pauses the nattuvangam for a split second, then resumes.*

ABI: What did you say?

SIVA: I said okay of course. [*To* GOWRIE] We're not using that land, let
them have it, no?

GOWRIE *wobbles her head in assent.*

Very good.

LAKSHMI *finally performs her dance movement correctly.*

LAKSHMI: Yes!

GOWRIE: See! You can do it if you just use your head properly.

LAKSHMI: Can I swim now?

KIDS: Swim! Swim!

GOWRIE: What is the necessity to swim?

LAKSHMI: We're walking to the beach!

GOWRIE: So? You should be studying. Even at the beach.

LAKSHMI: Appa's here so we can swim now! You said it this morning,
you said after dance class and when Appa comes back!

GOWRIE: I did / not.

KIDS: 'After dance class and not until Appa comes back from church.'

SIVA: That is true, see. I already have on my swimmers underneath my
pants.

He shows the top of his pants. The kids crack up.

GOWRIE: Chi! Silly man, you went to church in your swimming shorts?

ALL: Amma!

GOWRIE: Okay.

LAKSHMI: Thank / god—

KIDS: Yay!

MADHU *lobs the ball to* AHILAN *with her left hand.*

MADHU: Hey thumbi catch!

GOWRIE: Madhu! What have I told you about using your left hand?

MADHU: Amma!

AHILAN: Amma that's how she was born!

GOWRIE: Nonsense. You can train any hand. All the best neurosurgeons are right-handed.

SIVA: How could you possibly know that?

GOWRIE: Kulagesaram sir is right-handed. So was his father.

LAKSHMI: Right, so that's all doctors / then—

AHILAN: But akka is destined to open the batting for the Sri Lankan women's / cricket team—

GOWRIE: That is just a *hobby* darling—

MADHU: I don't want to be a neurosurgeon. I want to be a veterinary surgeon!

GOWRIE: A vet? Who wants to marry a vet? Will the house be full of monkeys?

MADHU: I love animals!

LAKSHMI: Do you think maybe Himal will be at the beach too?

AHILAN: Just passing by?

LAKSHMI: Passing by! Passing by!

Laughter from the kids. LAKSHMI *makes kissy-kissy gestures to* ABI—*she thinks her parents can't see.*

ABI: Stop it!

GOWRIE: Lakshmi! Don't be disgusting. Abi if I ever see you and Himal alone together I'll slap him all the way back to his father's house and you will never see each other again. Understood?

ABI: Yes, Amma. [*Whispering to Lakshmi*] / Idiot.

SIVA: Kishan uncle was at the church service this morning. I told him to bring Himal to the beach, yes.

He gives ABI *a friendly head wobble.*

But your Amma is right. There's a way to do these things, darling.

ABI: I know. Thank you / Appa.

GOWRIE: Isn't Himal's mother a Buddhist?

SIVA: Well Kishan's Singhalese. He married a Singhalese. And yes, she happens to be a Buddhist.

GOWRIE: Moorooha!

AHILAN: What's wrong with that, Amma? You're a Tamil Hindu and you married a Tamil Christian.

GOWRIE: Because, mahan, if Himal and Abi get married then we'll have to do the ceremony three times! One Christian, one Hindu, one Buddhist!

LAKSHMI: Four times!

SIVA: There she goes.

ABI: You just want to be an atheist because you think it's all cool / and western—

LAKSHMI: Shut up, Abi!

ABI: [*mimicking her*] 'Appa, can I go to Oxford University one day? I want to / be a lawyer—'

GOWRIE: [*smacking her head*] Abi!

LAKSHMI: I'm an atheist because I believe in logic. You all believe in different Gods. How can they all be true?

SIVA: Very good / point, Lakshmi.

GOWRIE: All paths lead to the same God, darling. Simple / no?

AHILAN: I think Muttiah Muralitharan is a God!

SIVA: Question! Can many different things be true at once?

A plane flies overhead and dozens of leaflets drop from above.

LAKSHMI, AHILAN *and* ABI *answer simultaneously.*

LAKSHMI: No!

AHILAN: Yes …

ABI: Depends.

MADHU: I don't think so …

SIVA *reads a leaflet.*

SIVA: 'Operation Leap Forward begins today. With God's help, we, the Government of Sri Lanka, will free the Sri Lankan Tamil people from the clutches of the brutal Liberation Tigers of Tamil Eelam.'

Beat.

So. It's happening.

ABI: Aren't we in a ceasefire?

LAKSHMI: Technically yes but the Tigers blew up three Sri Lankan navy boats—

ABI: So they're responding / with their own attack?

GOWRIE: Quiet!

SIVA: [*reading*] No darlings. This is different. The Sri Lankan Army want to occupy Jaffna. They want to take back the north from the Tigers. This time the army is coming up here to stay.

LAKSHMI: They're going to set up bases here?

SIVA: Yes darling. This is the beginning of something new.

MADHU: How long will they be staying for?

SIVA: I don't know, mahal.

LAKSHMI: [*reading*] They're calling it a 'war for peace'—

ABI: A war for / what?

AHILAN: Are they attacking our village?

SIVA: [*still studying the pamphlet*] No, mahan. They are attacking Valigamam and bombing near Palaly. But not here. Not in Navali.

AHILAN: Do we need to go to the bunkers?

SIVA: No no, they will not bomb here mahan. I will check with Kishan Uncle, he is a government officer now, but they will not bomb here, you see?

ABI: [*reading the pamphlet*] Yes, they're telling people up there to come and take refuge in churches and temples around here.

SIVA: Yes, so we will shelter them in Saint Peter's church and in our temple, okay?

KIDS: Okay Appa.

GOWRIE: I'll go back with the children and we'll get ready to take them in. / Come children, come come.

SIVA: Good, I will go to see Kishan. Go go go.

*

SIVA *hurries off and the rest of the family run home.*

A man, SALIM, *waits outside their house.*

GOWRIE: Mahal. Get our emergency bags from storage / and whatever bedsheets we have.

MADHU: Yes, Amma.

AHILAN: [*motioning to* SALIM] Amma.

SALIM: Gowrie-Amma.

GOWRIE: Salim? What are you doing here? If the Tigers see you—

SALIM: [*getting her blessings*] We still have business here. No-one knows we're Muslim, we just dress like Hindus and nobody notices

us. [*Holding up the leaflet*] I didn't know where else to go. I can't
go home now, the roads are blocked—
GOWRIE: Salim, it's okay. It's okay mahan. Come to the church with us …
SALIM: Gowrie-Amma. My wife, my baby— / they're here too—
GOWRIE: So go get them!
SALIM: Nandri, Amma.

 He leaves.

GOWRIE: Mahan, go get me some coconuts and the big bags of rice.
AHILAN: Yes Amma—
GOWRIE: Abi, get me some murunga and chillies from the garden, we
will make sambar rice.
ABI: Okay Amma.

 She goes.

 SIVA *and* KISHAN *enter.*

MADHU: Kishan uncle!
KISHAN: Hello cricketer.
SIVA: Kishan called Colombo.

 GOWRIE *helps* MADHU *fold bedsheets.*

KISHAN: It's okay. They are not bombing here. Not in Navali. Only near
Palaly. [*To* SIVA] Your church, [*to* GOWRIE] your temple. All okay.
Okay? I spoke to the guys in Colombo. All places of worship will
be safe.
MADHU: Thank you uncle.

 SALIM *returns with his wife,* WOMAN ONE, *who is cradling a baby.
Her sari is over her head like a hijab.* SALIM *is clutching his topi.*

SIVA: Lakshmi and Ahilan, people from Palaly are gathering at Ladies
College. Go tell them to come to either Saint Peter's Church or to
the temple. Salim, you can put your topi on and come to the church.
Everyone is gathered there.
SALIM: Thank you Siva.
KISHAN: I must—
SIVA: Of course, Kishan, go go go.
KISHAN: Can you send the children to Jeya Bakery, they have food ready
for the church?

GOWRIE: We will take care of it, you go go go.

> GOWRIE *begins to exit.*

Abi, where are the vegetables?

SIVA: Thank you, Kishan.

> GOWRIE *exits with a bag of coconuts and a tray.*

Madhu take them to the church. [*To* LAKSHMI *and* AHILAN] You, go go! I will go to Jeya Bakery.

> MADHU *and* SALIM *exit.*

KIDS: Yes Appa.

> LAKSHMI *and* AHILAN *exit.*
>
> SIVA *walks briskly.*
>
> *He stops and he looks overhead.*
>
> *There's a sound of a plane.*
>
> *He looks back towards the church, then breaks into a run towards the church.*

SIVA: Dear God!

> *Music plays and the revolve turns faster than* SIVA *can run.*

*

A shoe, lying on its side, turns on the revolve.

*

MADHU, *sitting in a chair, covered in dust.*

LAKSHMI *is with her.*

A SURGEON *bandages* MADHU*'s left hand.*

LAKSHMI: The church is just rubble. Some people could walk but not many—my brother carried her then went back with a tractor to bring more—the Red Cross are at church now but many more will still be coming—

SURGEON: How many?

LAKSHMI: More than a hundred. Maybe many more. I don't know. I don't know how many under the rubble. Many.

SURGEON: Okay.

> *He goes to exit.*

LAKSHMI: What about my sister?

SURGEON: We are just a teaching hospital, I cannot save it. I'll come back soon to amputate it. Very sorry.

*

SIVA, *sitting in a chair, covered in dust.*

GOWRIE *is with him.*

The SURGEON *examines his eyes.*

SURGEON: What can you see? Can you see anything?

SIVA: Cracks. A fine light and cracks. Like a spider web across everything.

SURGEON: Some blurring?

SIVA: Blurred light. Mostly black, but a little bit.

SURGEON: Across both eyes?

SIVA: Everything.

*

SALIM, *sitting in a chair, covered in dust.*

The SURGEON *examines* SALIM.

ABI *is there, writing down what the* SURGEON *says.*

SALIM *looks unharmed, but he responds to nothing.*

SURGEON: Bandages, antibiotics, butterfly clips, IV, painkillers, any kind, even paracetamol, but any kind. Syringes, gloves—just anything, anything at all. Do you have a car?

ABI: I will find one.

> SIVA *appears.*

SURGEON: And calipers. C-A-L-I-P-E—

SALIM: [*to* SIVA] You! My baby is dead because of you, you sent us to the church!

SALIM *attacks* SIVA.

It is your fault, your fault, your fault.

*

AHILAN *and* ABI.

AHILAN *is covered in dust.*

He washes his face as he talks.

AHILAN: The roof is gone—there are just holes in the walls—people are stuck under the rubble—we were pulling them out—I just brought twenty more on the tractor—there was a baby, maybe one year old— and the English teacher's wife—I forget her name—Thevayani?—she was still breathing at first—

LAKSHMI *enters.*

They look at her.

So?

LAKSHMI: They will amputate her left thumb.

AHILAN *exits, swearing profusely in Tamil.*

Ahilan!

*

ABI *finds* HIMAL.

ABI: Himal! Can you drive me into town?

HIMAL: Abi—

ABI: We need medical supplies. Antibiotics. Painkillers. I need Ventolin.

HIMAL: My father just told me he is sending me to Colombo. He says it's not safe for me to stay here in the north. I'm leaving.

Beat.

ABI: Okay.

She starts to leave.

I need to find a car, I need to find medical supplies—

HIMAL: Abi.

She stops.

I'll come back. You'll see.

ABI: Why? You are not a crazy person Himal.

HIMAL: No?

ABI: So don't be crazy.

Beat.

I have to go.

She goes.

HIMAL: Abi! I'll come back. I'll find you!

*

AHILAN *walks past objects strewn by the blast, swearing as he goes.*
A LTTE COMMANDER *joins him.*

COMMANDER: Brother.

AHILAN: [*in Tamil*] Fuck off.

COMMANDER: [*in Tamil*] Good. [*In English*] Very good. We need that anger. Let it out.

Beat.

Go on, let it out.

AHILAN: [*in Tamil*] FUCK YOU ALL.

He stops and bursts into tears. The COMMANDER *waits for* AHILAN *to settle.*

COMMANDER: You're in shock. But I expected this.

AHILAN: It was a church! Protected by God!

COMMANDER: I don't pretend to know about God. But I know about this world. I know how *this* place works.

Pause.

You are Siva and Gowrie's only son, Ahilan. You have three siblings. Abirami, Madhu, and Lakshmi.

AHILAN *realises who he's walking next to.*

AHILAN: You're wasting your time.

COMMANDER: You're the only son.

AHILAN: I'm not joining the Tigers.

COMMANDER: Join us and we won't ask any more of your family. We'll leave the others alone. I promise you.

AHILAN: I'm not joining the Tigers.

COMMANDER: We're not what you think we are.

AHILAN: When you were driving all the Muslims out of the north, my father stood up against you. He said, if they are finding excuses to drive *this* group out now, it'll be some *other* group next. We are only safe when everyone is safe.

COMMANDER: Do you still believe that? How do you think the families down south feel right now? Safe, I am sure. Very safe. But us?

AHILAN: The Red Cross were there. At the church. Not just helping. Recording. Taking pictures. Getting testimonies.

COMMANDER: We've been trying to get justice that way for *fifty years*.

AHILAN: We'll keep trying.

COMMANDER: How long do we have to try before you admit that it doesn't work? So far sixty-five bodies were found in the rubble of your church. How many more will they find tomorrow? Six babies, dead in their mother's arms. Like Salim, you know Salim? Yes? He attacked your father, no?

> *Beat.*

Why shouldn't he? It's people like your father—kind, open, compassionate—that are abused by the kind of people who end up in power. He called someone, no? Your father? Checked with someone when he read those leaflets?

> *Beat.*

Kishan. That Sinhala Government officer. You know why they bombed your father's church?

> *Beat.*

Because they wanted to send a signal—you are not welcome here. You will never be welcome here.

AHILAN: We have always been here.

COMMANDER: That's the genius of it. The way they make you doubt things you used to think were self-evident.

AHILAN: Perhaps a few are like that. But not all Sri Lankans—

COMMANDER: More than you would like to believe. And they are the ones that have the power—

AHILAN: Then we will get it back! *All* Sri Lankans. The people / must get the power back—

COMMANDER: Power is not just given *freely*, Ahilan. Stop thinking like your father! Power must be *taken*. By force, if necessary. It has always been that way. Your father's truth is how we *want* the world to be. Myself included. I wish it was that way. But what I am telling you now is how the world *really is*. Becoming an adult is learning not to confuse the two. Are you listening?

AHILAN *is listening.*

Your father, your mother, they can leave if they want to. You are vellalas. Landowners. Your caste, you can all leave whenever you want to. But I can't. My family can't. Most of our people can't. Our only choice is to defend ourselves. To keep what is ours, before we lose it. That's all we are asking for. To keep what is already ours. Our homeland. If you really want to help, to do something useful, then you need to work with us.

The COMMANDER *starts to exit.*

Come. You don't have to make your mind up immediately. Just come. And let me teach you more about what we do. Or you can go back into that teaching hospital and dream about your 'justice'.

AHILAN *stands. The* COMMANDER *waits, about to exit.*

AHILAN: My mother will never let me go.

*

GOWRIE, ABI *and* LAKSHMI *are packing bags.*

MADHU *and* SIVA *sit, unable to do anything. Madhu's hand is bandaged.*

LAKSHMI *is on the phone as she packs.*

ABI: [*to* GOWRIE] They want us to go. The government wants people like you and Appa to leave the country.

LAKSHMI: [*on the phone*] No aunty, just the visas …

GOWRIE: [*handing* ABI *items to pack*] Take this.

LAKSHMI: I can fax our ID cards to you from the Navali post office—

ABI: [*to* SIVA] If you go to Australia, they win. Every Tamil, gone from Sri Lanka.

LAKSHMI: [*to the others*] Malini Mami says you can watch every game of the world cup next year on the big TV in her house.

ABI: Appa!

LAKSHMI: And she says you can drink water from the tap and on the weekend, after temple, you can go to the beach and there's no rubbish.

ABI: [*sarcastically*] Oh yay Australia.

> *The* LTTE COMMANDER *enters and walks into the middle of the room. He pays his respects to* GOWRIE *and* SIVA.

LAKSHMI: Yes, thank you, Malini Mami— / Yes—

COMMANDER: Gowrie-Amma. You are leaving, no? Have you asked your Sinhala Government friend to help you? Siva-Appa. Did he tell you, 'Yes, please, send everybody to the church, very safe, very safe.' Your Sinhala friend?

> *He gives* ABI *a note.*

> LAKSHMI *hangs up the phone.*

> GOWRIE *walks to the* COMMANDER.

GOWRIE: Give me back my son.

ABI: Amma—

COMMANDER: He's not mine to give back.

GOWRIE: I want to talk to my son, now.

COMMANDER: Ahilan specifically asked me *not* to let you talk to him, Gowrie-Amma. Please. Read the note.

> GOWRIE *looks at* ABI *and gestures 'what is it'.*

ABI: It's Ahilan's writing.

LAKSHMI: What does it say?

ABI: [*reading*] Moorooha.

LAKSHMI: What does it say!

GOWRIE: Read it!

ABI: 'Lakshmi was right. There is no God. Do not come looking for me. I made this choice.'

> *Pause.*

GOWRIE: Ahilan is a kind boy. He is a good boy. You have abused that goodness.

COMMANDER: [*pointing again at* SIVA] With the greatest respect, Gowrie-Amma. Look where your goodness got you.

GOWRIE: [*walking up to the* COMMANDER] Hear my words, young man. One day, when you least expect it, my son's kindness will be your undoing. It will lead to your death. And I will not grieve over your body.

    Beat.

COMMANDER: As I told your son, Gowrie-Amma, I don't pretend to know about these things. Fate. Destiny. But whatever happens to me, I know this: I doubt very much it is you who gets to decide.

    The COMMANDER *leaves.*

    Silence.

    ABI *goes to leave.*

ABI: I'll follow him and find thumbi—

SIVA: No!

LAKSHMI: [*grabbing her*] Abi-Akka!

ABI: [*shoving her back*] What is your problem?

LAKSHMI: So you're going to pick a fight with the Tigers as well?

ABI: I'm not just going to do what they tell us to do!

LAKSHMI: They already want our parents dead for criticising them in public. The government wants to kill us for being Tamil. Our village wants to blame us because we have Sinhala friends. Salim already attacked Appa.

ABI: Maybe Kishan did know, huh?

LAKSHMI: What?

ABI: He works for the government! They sent people to shelter in the church and then they bombed the church!

LAKSHMI: Abi!

GOWRIE: I am not leaving Sri Lanka without my son.

    Pause.

LAKSHMI: Amma. It is not safe for us to stay in Sri Lanka anymore. We have to leave.

MADHU: Amma, I will go and meet the Tiger boys at Jeya Bakery. They'll feel sorry for me, they'll tell me where thumbi is / —let me go and ask—

LAKSHMI: They won't feel sorry for you. They will point to you and say, 'Stupid girl whose father gathered everyone in the church.'

ABI: Amma we know those boys from school—

LAKSHMI: It is different now.

MADHU: This is our village.

LAKSHMI: Not anymore.

ABI: It is still our village. I will go to those boys, we will find thumbi and bring him back.

LAKSHMI: Amma! Anna is already gone. He is already on a truck. Already in the jungle. Tigers have him! Appa!

SIVA: We failed, darling. It is as simple as that. I cannot stay. But I cannot leave my son.

GOWRIE: Lakshmi. Take Appa to Australia. Abi. This afternoon, go to Jeya Bakery and ask the boys where Ahilan is going to be stationed. Take Madhu with you. Wherever Ahilan goes, we will follow and bring him back.

LAKSHMI: Amma?

GOWRIE: Siva?

> SIVA *wobbles his head, yes.*

SIVA: Yes, alright …

ABI: [*to* LAKSHMI] Take Appa to Australia. Go with him. We'll find thumbi, then we'll come and join you. Okay?

LAKSHMI: Amma …

SIVA: Oh.

LAKSHMI: What?

SIVA: That was it. The last of the light. The last little crack.

MADHU: What do you see now? Black?

SIVA: Not black. Just … nothing. It's like trying to look behind you by facing the front.

> *Beat.*

GOWRIE: Ahilan is only a boy. A boy who wants to be a man. When I should have been there, I was not. And another man came and convinced him he was a Tiger.

MADHU: Amma, this is not your fault—

GOWRIE: Yes it is. Mine, and Appa's. It is our duty as parents to protect our children. And we failed.

> GOWRIE *rips a piece of her saree and ties it around her eyes, as a blindfold.*

I will not remove this until all of my children are together with me again.

The revolve turns.

ABI, MADHU *and* GOWRIE *assemble on one side;* LAKSHMI *and* SIVA *assemble on the other.*

We move through time:

*

ABI, MADHU *and* GOWRIE *take a truck to the Vanni as bombs fall around them.*

LAKSHMI *and* SIVA *take a plane to Australia.*

*

AHILAN *is given his LTTE uniform and gun by the* COMMANDER. AHILAN *receives the objects with respect. The* COMMANDER *treats him like a son.*

*

ABI, MADHU *and* GOWRIE *start farming a tiny plot of land in the Vanni. Years pass.*

*

AHILAN, *now dressed as a LTTE soldier, learns medical skills from the* COMMANDER.

*

A small plastic toy pink flamingo revolves on the stage.

GOWRIE, ABI *and* MADHU *argue about the flamingo.*

The women travel to Chundikulam National Park.

ABI *confronts a* LTTE SOLDIER *there about Ahilan's whereabouts, but he respectfully ignores her. She gets up to attack him, and* MADHU *drags her away.*

*

LAKSHMI, *in an Australian school uniform, tosses a netball around. She brings* SIVA *a copy of braille solitaire.*

*

AHILAN, *dressed as a LTTE soldier, learns farming skills from the* COMMANDER.

*

GOWRIE, ABI *and* MADHU *ride in a truck.*
A conch revolves on the stage.
GOWRIE, ABI *and* MADHU *argue about the conch.*

*

LAKSHMI, *in a Red Rooster uniform, brings home some fast food for her and* SIVA *to eat. She shows him a song on her discman headphones. She has study books.*

*

GOWRIE, ABI *and* MADHU *ride in a truck.*
HIMAL *walks by, holding a chicken.* MADHU *notices him first—she tells* ABI.
GOWRIE, ABI *and* MADHU *all try to get off the truck and reunite with* HIMAL—*the group splits and they run off in different directions.*

*

LAKSHMI *enters, well dressed, wearing a graduation hat. She helps* SIVA *put on a nice jacket.*

*

The revolve continues to turn.

ACT TWO

Sydney, 2009.

LAKSHMI *(early 30s)* and SIVA *(early 50s) are having dinner at Bennelong at the Opera House. Lakshmi's graduation hat is on the table.*

SIVA *is blind.*

SIVA: Yes but you could just put me in a taxi—
LAKSHMI: Why are you still talking about this?
SIVA: —and then I call out that Ravi fellow next door—
LAKSHMI: We're here now, Appa, it's my decision—
SIVA: —and he comes and takes me into the apartment—
LAKSHMI: Are you even listening to me at all?
SIVA: —it's not difficult for me and it's better for you, [*angrily*] I mean, honestly! For god's sake, Lakshmi!
LAKSHMI: What? What are you telling me off for! I'm telling you off!
SIVA: What for? Why didn't you go out with your friends / instead of taking your boring father out for dinner!
LAKSHMI: I wanted to take you out for dinner!

> SIVA *doesn't hear her.*

SIVA: What?
LAKSHMI: Because I wanted to take you out— Why did I bother?
SIVA: My question exactly! All your friends have gone out to celebrate / and instead you are sitting here arguing—
LAKSHMI: I want to celebrate with you. Instead I am sitting here—yes— arguing with you, yes.
SIVA: Yes exactly! Better to go with your friends!
LAKSHMI: Yeah!
SIVA: Yes!
LAKSHMI: YES!
SIVA: So what is the problem?
LAKSHMI: You—
Appa—
Just—
Sssssshhhhhhh! I have brought you to Bennelong. It's a very

expensive restaurant. We are inside the Opera House. There is a view of the Harbour Bridge. Here is tiny, expensive food. It's *my* graduation. It's *my* treat. It's already happening so stop trying to get out of it and drink your wine and celebrate, your daughter is a lawyer, okay?

SIVA: They brought the wine already, why didn't you tell me?

LAKSHMI: Because I wanted to throw it at you. Here.

SIVA: Are you wearing your graduation hat?

LAKSHMI: [*lying*] Yes Appa.

> *They clink their glasses and take a sip.*

SIVA: Congratulations darling.

> LAKSHMI *begins to eat—*

Why don't you let that Ravi boy take you out for dinner?

LAKSHMI: [*sighing; she knows full well who he is*] Who?

SIVA: *Ravi.* The neighbour who keeps coming over to borrow our tomato sauce.

LAKSHMI: You think Ravi wants to ask me out?

SIVA: Well I'm far from an expert in these things, but it seems to me that no-one eats *that* much tomato sauce, darling, and if they *did*, they would most certainly buy it themselves—

LAKSHMI: Appa—

SIVA: What? Is he not attractive? He has a very nice voice—

LAKSHMI: I don't—Appa—I'm not—

SIVA: What?

> *Beat.*

LAKSHMI: I don't like Ravis.

> *Beat.*

SIVA: That's a bit odd, kunju. What about that other fellow from the graduation ceremony who asked you to a drink? He's not called Ravi, is he?

LAKSHMI: Did you want a tiny little entree with mushrooms or a tiny little entree with … scallops, I think.

SIVA: Can't I have both?

LAKSHMI: You can't have both!

SIVA: You have to explain to me darling, how you are going to get married if you don't spend more time with other people. Four years of a law degree, everywhere every day all around you are future boys to be lawyers, not a single date with any of them.

LAKSHMI: Why are you acting like Amma all of a sudden? Have you been saving it all up until I graduate?

SIVA: If you only take *me* to restaurants you will end up marrying a waiter.

LAKSHMI: I'm not marrying anyone! Okay?! Just eat.

SIVA: Darling. I have my own problems.

LAKSHMI: What does that mean?

SIVA: You know very well what that means.

> *Beat.*

LAKSHMI: I saw the same things you saw.

SIVA: And whose fault is that? The only reason people gathered in that church was because of me.

LAKSHMI: What? No. Appa—

SIVA: If I must sink, then let me sink kunju. Don't come down with me.

LAKSHMI: Appa. It wasn't your fault. You know that, don't you? It wasn't your fault.

SIVA: Kunju. It's my right to choose how I feel about what happened. I can't come to terms with it. I never will.

LAKSHMI: It was fifteen years ago. We have a new life now—

SIVA: No. *You* have your whole life ahead of you. Not me.

LAKSHMI: We both do, Appa! You just need to get out of the house a little more—

SIVA: Where would I go?

LAKSHMI: The Tamil Association—

SIVA: They don't trust me—

LAKSHMI: The Singhalese Association—

SIVA: Highly suspicious of me—

LAKSHMI: You're making this difficult on purpose.

SIVA: How will you find a boy if you only ever spend time studying or at work or with me in our tiny apartment? I have to let go of you—let you be free. For heaven's sake, Lakshmi, do I have to force you—

LAKSHMI: [*quietly*] I have found someone.

SIVA: What?

LAKSHMI: Forget it.

SIVA: Just talk to me, kunju. I've been through everything already.

Pause.

LAKSHMI: I don't like Ravis, Appa. I like Vaishnavis. And Natalies. And Claudia.

Pause.

SIVA: Really, darling?

LAKSHMI: Yes.

SIVA: I really must have both entrees now.

LAKSHMI: You just said you'd be okay with this!

SIVA: I am, I just didn't—I need some time darling—

LAKSHMI: Oh my god. I'm not … I'm still trying to figure it out myself.

SIVA: Good! So why don't you take that Ravi boy out / for dinner just one time—

LAKSHMI: No, sorry, that's not true. I've always known.

Beat.

I'm in love, Appa. I am in love with a woman. Her name is Claudia. We met at uni. And actually—I think you'd really like her.

Pause.

SIVA: Is this because you are Australian now?

LAKSHMI: Appa!

SIVA: You know, kunju. I try to be very accepting. When you told me you were an atheist, I accepted it.

LAKSHMI: Yes—

SIVA: But a 'lesbian' atheist? A straight atheist, okay. A lesbian person of faith, okay. But a lesbian atheist. I mean, / really darling that's not fair—

LAKSHMI: When I told you that I didn't believe in God—

SIVA: You had very good reasons—

LAKSHMI: —you encouraged me to be who I am.

SIVA: Yes.

LAKSHMI: Even though it would be difficult. I mean come on Appa, I was probably the only atheist in Jaffna. I'm hardly the only lesbian in Sydney.

SIVA: You were questioning the world. Of course I would support that. This is different, darling—

LAKSHMI: No, Appa. It's not. It's who I am. You have always encouraged me to be who I am. And this is who I am.

Long pause.

SIVA: 'Love bears all things.'

LAKSHMI: You haven't quoted from the Bible in fifteen years.

SIVA: I'm surprised you know what I'm quoting.

LAKSHMI: I have to know what I'm disagreeing with, don't I?

SIVA: That is absolutely correct.

LAKSHMI: 'Love bears all things, believes all things, hopes all things, / endures all things.'

SIVA: 'Endures all things.'

We have not been kind to love, darling. Those of us who have loved before you. We have abused it, betrayed it, sensationalised it, become intoxicated with it. And yet it endures us. This love. God has given it to all of us, no? How can such a force be only for some of us? All I ask is that you be kind to it. Be better to it than we have been before you … It doesn't matter … who you love, darling. So much as *how* you love them.

Pause.

LAKSHMI: So …

SIVA: Okay.

LAKSHMI: Okay?

SIVA: Okay.

LAKSHMI: Okay.

SIVA: Ah no, not okay—

LAKSHMI: What?!

SIVA: What about grandchildren?! I forgot about grandchildren!

LAKSHMI: For god's sake. I can still have children, Appa—

SIVA: You can? Now *that* is an Australian / thing, yes—

LAKSHMI: No! Oh my god—

SIVA: Then what is it—

LAKSHMI: There's a number of ways … we can involve … a man, or … use an … implement to put the, ah—

SIVA: Ah. No thank you. / That's enough.

LAKSHMI: You asked.

SIVA: Very good. I have enough information now.

LAKSHMI: Fine.

Beat.

SIVA: [*in Tamil first, then in English*] You mean everything to me. [*In English*] I love you mahal. I love you first, and whatever comes after that, must come after that, I suppose. My atheist, Australian, lesbian daughter.

LAKSHMI: Thank you, Appa.

SIVA: No thank *you*, for being so patient with me.

LAKSHMI: Love is for all of us Appa. Yes? Even you.

She takes his hand.

Beat.

It was not your fault.

Beat.

Do you want to get out of here Appa, get some dosai?

SIVA: Very good idea darling. These entrees are far too tiny.

LAKSHMI: Excellent. [*Looking for her keys*] Where are my …

She starts searching through her bag.

Oh. I can't find my keys …

SIVA *draws them out from behind her ears.*

SIVA: They were hiding in your ears, darling. How strange.

LAKSHMI: Oh my god.

SIVA: You really should clean them more often.

LAKSHMI: Seriously Appa, I'm not a kid / anymore—

SIVA: Do you want me to have fun or not, because you can't have it both ways.

She tickles him.

Lakshmi! You would tickle a blind man? Have you no decorum?

Lakshmi's phone dings with a new message.

Ah! That must be the poor thing not named Ravi hoping you will have a drink with them—

LAKSHMI: [*reading, concernedly*] It's Abi.

*

SIVA *and* LAKSHMI *are in their kitchen.*

LAKSHMI *is manically scrolling on her phone.*

LAKSHMI: They were going to take the A-thirty-five, towards Suthanthirapuram—there is bombing all around them, fighting—the president has declared a no-fire zone inside the Tamil Tiger areas, behind the front lines, but it's hard to know what's—the Sri Lankan Army and the Tigers are cornering hundreds of thousands of Tamil civilians—there are no journalists, the UN are leaving—just bits on the internet, Twitter—no way to know what's real, what's gossip, lies—

SIVA: Darling—

LAKSHMI: [*putting her phone on the table*] She said she would message again when she found a generator to charge her phone, but it's been ... three days.

SIVA: Kunju—

LAKSHMI: [*distractedly*] Hmm?

SIVA: Darling calm down, sit down ...

She sits.

She gets back up again and goes to put her shoes on.

LAKSHMI: I'm going out. There are protests in Martin Place.

Beat.

SIVA: Darling—Kunju.

LAKSHMI: What? / What?

SIVA: Just ... Listen to me. Who is protesting?

LAKSHMI: What do you mean, who is protesting? Sri Lankans.

SIVA: Sri Lankans. Really?

LAKSHMI: Yes really. Tamil Sri Lankans.

SIVA: Tamil Sri Lankans calling for a separate Tamil homeland—

LAKSHMI: Yes! Not just here but in Chennai, Toronto, London—

SIVA: Waving blood-red flags with a growling Tiger and an AK-forty-seven asking for peace.

LAKSHMI: We are angry. We want justice.

SIVA: I am angry. I want justice. But that means thinking first.

LAKSHMI: Oh thinking, always thinking. You have been thinking for fifteen years—what has that achieved? Nothing. It has achieved nothing. You have achieved nothing.

SIVA: Lakshmi, that is … That is not a dignified argument.

LAKSHMI: This is the President of Sri Lanka: 'If you are not willing to accept the fact that we are not using heavy weapons, I really can't help it. We are not using heavy weapons.' They are using heavy weapons! On their own citizens! There is satellite imagery. Our family are in that hell. And you want to have a dignified argument. Don't be insulting. I am going to the protest.

She goes.

*

LAKSHMI *and* SIVA *sit at the kitchen table.*

LAKSHMI *is scrolling through photos on the internet.*

LAKSHMI: They're bombing the hospital in PTK. Is that something they do then?

SIVA: Darling—

LAKSHMI: Set up a safe area, and then bomb it.

Rows and rows of white tents.

Burnt out buses and lorries.

Lines and lines and lines of people.

Huh. A makeshift school. Still teaching the children. Is that Father? From Navali? Appa? You can't tell me. I don't know.

Another burnt out bus. A truck.

Lakshmi's phone rings.

LAKSHMI *snatches it up.*

Abi?

Beat.

No, I do not have five minutes to provide you with feedback on your customer service. Do not call me again.

Beat.

DO NOT CALL ME AGAIN. DO NOT CALL ME AGAIN.

She throws her phone back on the table and gets up.

Do you want a cup of tea?

*

SIVA *and* LAKSHMI *are in the kitchen.*

LAKSHMI *is scrolling through her phone.*

LAKSHMI: They've herded one hundred thousand people onto a tiny beach between the ocean and Nanthikkadal Lagoon. They are shelling them with weapons intended to destroy concrete and tanks. Dead bodies. Dead children. Dead women. Living bodies. Trucks. Buses. Sleeping mats. Cooking fires. Blankets. Like they have picked up a town and tipped it all out onto a beach. Appa I have to go to Sri Lanka.

> *Pause.*

I am going back to / Sri Lanka.

SIVA: Yes I know.

> *Beat.*

I know you will go, I know why you will go. I'll call Kishan. He will organise it. Go to the bank, take out all our savings, put it inside your toiletries bag, keep it with you. Take your Australian passport.

> *She hurries to start packing.*

Lakshmi. Make sure you come back. Bring them all back. Make sure you come back. Lakshmi?

LAKSHMI: I will.

SIVA: Say it, would you?

LAKSHMI: What?

SIVA: Promise me.

LAKSHMI: I promise I will come back with our family.

ACT THREE

The Vanni, 2009.

We pick up with ABI, MADHU, GOWRIE *and* HIMAL *at the exact moment we last saw them.* GOWRIE *remains blindfolded.*

We move through time:

HIMAL *tries to reunite with* ABI, MADHU *and* GOWRIE. *He makes repeated attempts to join the family but* ABI *rejects him.*

With Madhu's support, HIMAL *eventually proves his commitment to* ABI *and their small-scale farming lifestyle, and joins the family.*

Years pass.

A plane flies overhead and drops leaflets.

ABI *picks up a leaflet.*

ABI: Here we go again. [*Reading*] 'Dear Citizen of the Vanni: we are launching a final war to liberate the people in the Vanni who have been suffering from the LTTE's ruthless terrorist acts. We, the Government of Sri Lanka, are doing our best to avoid the human casualties of war. Therefore, we are requesting you, the beloved Tamils, to leave the Tiger-controlled territories and come immediately into government-liberated areas to protect yourself from this disaster.'

    Pause.

Last time was the beginning. Now it is the beginning of the end.

MADHU: A final war?

ABI: Yes.

MADHU: [*in disbelief*] An end to war.

ABI: It is almost a relief. Fifteen years we have hacked away at the jungle, built houses where no-one was supposed to live, we have not seen our brother, our sister, our father. Twenty-six years of two countries, two peoples. Sinhala, Tamil. Government, LTTE. *They* don't just bomb our fighters; they bomb our houses and our neighbours—they bomb our fish traps, schools, farms. *We* don't just shoot back at our oppressors—we shoot our own teachers, priests, doctors. *They* will do anything to win, and so *we* will do anything to win. I thought it would go on for ever. But now it seems it will soon come to an end. [*To* MADHU] But don't try and imagine a life after this. Not yet. Too much to happen first. We must live through it. But the end has begun.

HIMAL: Marry me.

ABI: Huh? What? What did I just say?

HIMAL: Marry me now. Then we can leave here.

ABI: You are Sinhala. The Tigers will let you leave. The government's soldiers will protect you. Go.

HIMAL: This is my family now. My father and mother will not speak to me again.

GOWRIE: Your mother will take you in her arms and will not let you go again.

ABI: There, listen to my mother, yes? They will take you back.

HIMAL: I made my choice when I came to the Vanni to find you. We will marry today.

ABI: Marriage is for after war.

HIMAL: I love you today.

ABI: A storm is coming, better to get away when you can. The Tigers will let you go so go, just go! Madhu, tell him some sense.

MADHU: Himal, marry my sister.

ABI: That is not what I said!

HIMAL: Madhu, find someone to marry us.

MADHU: Yes!

ABI: You are a Buddhist. Where is there a Buddhist priest in the Vanni now?

HIMAL: I will marry like a Hindu. Find a priest. Any priest.

FATHER JAMES *walks past.*

MADHU: Any priest? [*Gesturing to* FATHER JAMES] This priest? A Catholic priest?

HIMAL: He is a priest? [*To* ABI] You see, it was meant to be.

MADHU: [*calling to* FATHER JAMES] Excuse me, Father James?

FATHER JAMES: Madhu. My child. How are you?

MADHU: [*to* GOWRIE] It is Father James, Amma. From my local church.

FATHER JAMES: Hello, Mrs Siva.

HIMAL: Sir, will you conduct a wedding for a Hindu and a Buddhist?

Beat.

FATHER JAMES: Do you think that is a good idea?

HIMAL: It is a very Sri Lankan idea.

FATHER JAMES: Okay I see your point. May I ask, who is getting married?

MADHU: Father James, it is my sister Abi, to this man, Himal. Childhood sweethearts.

FATHER JAMES: Mrs Siva?

GOWRIE: They love each other. They always have.

ABI: Amma!

FATHER JAMES: Then I will make a wedding.

HIMAL: Abi?

> *Beat.*

GOWRIE: Wedding or not, child? Now or maybe never.

> *Beat.*

ABI: [*to* HIMAL] I shall make the decisions.

HIMAL: I like your decisions.

ABI: We will live in the north.

HIMAL: I came back here. I will stay here.

ABI: One day we will have a home that we will never leave. We will grow a mango tree and pawpaws and karivapillai and dry chillies on the porch and chase our chickens across our paddy fields. And our children will be born into a home they will never be forced to leave.

HIMAL: Yes.

> *Beat.*

ABI: If Amma says yes, then yes, marry me, idiot, but it is on your head.

HIMAL: Gowrie-Amma?

GOWRIE: Yes already.

HIMAL: Thank you. Father, please.

FATHER JAMES: Madhu, child, run and get my Bible and my stole from the church.

MADHU: Yes!

> MADHU *runs out.*

> GOWRIE *begins weaving together some simple garlands.*

FATHER JAMES: What is your name, sir?

HIMAL: Himal.

FATHER JAMES: Himal, my friend, please write down a Buddhist verse by which you will live your lives together.

HIMAL: Yes Father.

FATHER JAMES: Child, what is your name?

ABI: Abirami.

FATHER JAMES: Abirami, tell me, please, because even in Sri Lanka this makes not very much sense. How did this come about?

ABI: How did you come about exactly at the moment my future husband magically needed a priest to pull off this trick?

FATHER JAMES: I was on my way to call a bishop in Toronto who says he knows how to get foreign journalists into the Vanni.

ABI: There you go, instead of getting foreign journalists into the Vanni you are marrying a Hindu and a Buddhist. You see, anything can happen any which way at any which moment. The reasons are not for us to know.

FATHER JAMES: Did you know I knew your father?

Beat.

GOWRIE: That shut her up, she who always knows everything.

FATHER JAMES: We were altar boys together in Navali. Your father always wanted to become a priest and I always wanted to have a lot of children. Instead it turns out that I am a priest and your father has a lot of children. Where is your father?

ABI: Guildford, Australia.

FATHER JAMES: Why am I not in Guildford, Australia? Why is it not your father who is interrupted on his way to make a phone call to invent a new kind of wedding? The tricky laws by which one person is fortunate and another is not. Why and how. This is my favourite topic.

In the distance, shelling begins.

ABI: They have started shelling.

MADHU *returns with the stole and the Bible.*

It is now dark.

A quiet, delicate ceremony begins, lit by a single lamp.

MADHU: Let's do it!

FATHER JAMES: Okay?

HIMAL: Okay.

ABI: Okay.

MADHU: Okay.

FATHER JAMES: I will sit. May I?

MADHU: Yes!

FATHER JAMES: [*handing the Bible to* MADHU] Read here.

MADHU: 'What of prophecies? They all come to an end. What of our tongues? They will cease talking. What of knowledge? It is finite. Only love does not insist on its own way. Love bears all things, believes all things, hopes all things, endures all things.'

　　　Distant shelling.

　　Appa's favourite.

FATHER JAMES: Yes. What next? Himal.

HIMAL: [*handing* FATHER JAMES *a piece of worn pamphlet*] From the Brahmajala Sutta. The words of our Buddha.

FATHER JAMES: I take up the way of not speaking falsely.

ABI *and* HIMAL: I take up the way of not speaking falsely.

FATHER JAMES: I take up the way of not killing.

ABI *and* HIMAL: I take up the way of not killing.

FATHER JAMES: I take up the way of not taking anything that is not given.

ABI *and* HIMAL: I take up the way of not taking anything that is not given.

FATHER JAMES: [*to* HIMAL] You read this bit.

　　　The kerosene lamp is passed to HIMAL.

HIMAL: 'When finally—'

　　　Distant shelling.

　　'When finally, nothing more can be done, that is where everything is. The great brightness. The truth, ready to harvest. Grasp it too tightly and you kill it; hold it with open hands and you follow the way of all Buddhas.'

FATHER JAMES: Very good. Mrs Siva?

MADHU: What about something for our sister Lakshmi?

FATHER JAMES: She is not Hindu?

ABI: Atheist.

FATHER JAMES: Dear God, I have nothing for her.

ABI: She is in Australia, she has everything.

FATHER JAMES: Ah!

FATHER JAMES *speaks a few lines of Joni Mitchell's 'Stardust'.*

ABI: Very good. What is it?

MADHU: Sounds very old.

FATHER JAMES: Joni Mitchell. 1969. Very good song.

Distant shelling.

ABI *and* HIMAL *repeat a line from Father James' quotation.*

Very good. [*To* GOWRIE] My Hindu friend?

GOWRIE *gives* HIMAL *and* ABI *garlands.*

On one garland is the pink flamingo.

On another is the conch shell.

A little unusual.

MADHU: [*to* FATHER JAMES] From our brother Ahilan. We think.

GOWRIE: Who else could it be?

MADHU: Twice now a package has come to us; inside a single object. To tell us he is alive.

GOWRIE: To tell us where he is.

MADHU: *Phoenicopterus roseus.* Flamingo. You find them in Chundikulam National Park.

ABI: We went to Chundikulam but LTTE told us nothing.

MADHU: This conch shell. *Turbinella pyrum pyrum.* They are everywhere in Sri Lanka.

ABI: He could be anywhere.

GOWRIE: Okay, enough. Three times.

She gives ABI *and* HIMAL *the garlands.*

The bride and groom garland each other three times.

MADHU *cracks open a coconut.*

GOWRIE *sings and gives them her blessings.*

Okay.

FATHER JAMES: I think you are married. Four times in one.

HIMAL: Aren't you supposed to say something official? 'I declare' or something?

FATHER JAMES: Ah … Himal and Abirami I pronounce you husband and wife.

MADHU: Amen.

ABI: Okay. [*In Tamil*] Very good.

HIMAL: Yes.

ABI: Very good.

HIMAL: [*in Sinhala*] Very very good. [*In English*] Yes very.

A moment of happiness.

HIMAL *wipes away tears.*

ABI: Don't cry.

HIMAL: I'm not sad. I'm happy.

ABI: But you are sad. You have crossed sides in a war to marry me.

HIMAL: There are no sides.

GOWRIE: [*touching him on the cheek*] You are my son now.

ABI: See, Amma, now you can say that at least one of your useless children finally got married.

The sound of bombs nearby.

GOWRIE: What do we do now?

HIMAL: We leave here. Away from the front line.

MADHU: No, we have already left one home, now another one? Do we always keep leaving?

HIMAL: What choice do we have?

ABI: Any little choice I will take it. Any bit of decision I will have it. They will bomb the paddy fields? Okay, I will choose to leave and find our brother.

MADHU: Akka, we have a good life here. We have built it ourselves and we have lived with bombs falling for fifteen years. We can stay.

More bombs sound nearby.

ABI: Thangacci, this is our home land, but it is not our home. This too like the one before it has become a place for war. Our home is still to come. Bring seeds. Bring the chicken. Bring the husband. Live longer than the war. Maybe find our brother. Then we will make a home. *Yes* we will have paddy fields. *Yes* we will dry chillies on the porch. Whatever it is, it is up to us. Nothing because of no. Only *yes*. But first we have to live. Thangacci?

Beat.

MADHU: Amma?

Beat.

GOWRIE: Yes, we live. We go.

Beat.

HIMAL: Shall we try and cross over into the government-controlled areas?

MADHU: The Sri Lankan Army is coming at us from the north, from the south and from the west. You want to cross to them, you must walk through the war.

ABI: Yes. This we know.

MADHU: And what would the army do with us if we did get there?

ABI: This we don't know.

MADHU: And will the Tigers even let us go?

ABI: No.

HIMAL: Why?

ABI: Who are they fighting for, if we all go?

Beat.

HIMAL: So we retreat with the Tigers?

ABI: Yes. Away from the front lines. Away from the war coming from the north, the south and the west. Tomorrow morning we go to the A-thirty-five Highway and we follow it east.

GOWRIE: And we will find Ahilan.

ABI: Yes.

FATHER JAMES: I have a Bishop in Toronto waiting for my call.

ABI: Of course. Thank you, Father.

HIMAL: Thank you.

MADHU: Bless you, Father.

FATHER JAMES: God bless you all. Goodbye. Good luck. Mrs Siva. May you be fortunate. And perhaps I will see you again.

*

Morning.

They walk.

Each of them carries their life in a bag.

MADHU *carries Himal's chicken in a basket.*

ABI: Highway, Amma—A-thirty-five Highway. No cars, many many many people, mostly walking. Many carts. Some buses. No soldiers.

A UN WORKER *joins them.*

MADHU: Where is everybody going?

UN WORKER: There is a safe zone. No-fire zone with the UN. It will be safe there. [*To* HIMAL *and* MADHU] Biscuit?

MADHU: No, thank you.

UN WORKER: I am UN. Local staff. Stay with me. [*To* GOWRIE *and* ABI] You want a biscuit?

ABI: No, thank you. [*Describing to the blindfolded* GOWRIE; *this act of description repeats throughout*] A nice man from the UN, Amma. An armchair in the middle of the road.

MADHU: I thought the UN had left?

UN WORKER: Yes and no.

MADHU: Yes and no?

UN WORKER: The government says they 'cannot guarantee the safety of humanitarian workers in final stage of a war', so all the UN international staff pulled out. Gone home. Only two left. Germans. Maybe Dutch. Or Swedish. Who can tell? Blond hair. So okay, there are still [*indicating himself*] many local staff. But oh sorry, no government doesn't want UN observers observing the war. So government has declared all UN staff 'on leave', therefore UN staff in the middle of the war cannot observe the war, because all UN staff are on leave. But then a different problem LTTE does not want any Tamil people to leave, so Tamil UN local staff on leave [*indicating himself*] cannot leave. So. We will all go to the UN hub in the no-fire zone. East. In Suthanthirapuram. We have sent coordinates of the hub to the Sri Lankan Army so they will not bomb. Should all be okay. You don't want biscuit?

ABI: No thank you. Shops all empty. Houses all empty. So many people.

GOWRIE *nods.*

There's a sound of a bird.

MADHU: Devil bird!

GOWRIE: Aanthi.

She makes the sign of the evil eye.

UN WORKER: Spot-bellied eagle owl.

MADHU: *Bubo nipalensis blighi.*

HIMAL: One of you must be right.

UN WORKER: [*laughing*] We are all right. [*To* MADHU] You know this genus? Cousin species to the barred eagle-owl, *Bubo sumatransis?*

MADHU: *Bubo sumatranus.*

UN WORKER: Really?

MADHU: Yes, really!

UN WORKER: Okay very good. You are …?

MADHU: No, just an amateur. [*Showing him a book in her bag*] *Helm's Field Guide.*

UN WORKER: Ah. I was a biologist once.

MADHU: Really?

UN WORKER: But I couldn't keep up my research during the war.

> *He shrugs.*

Now I recite the names to distract myself when I am waiting at checkpoints. *Tyto alba stertens.*

MADHU: Barn owl. Easy one! *Otus thilohoffmanni.*

UN WORKER: Ah. Serendib Scops Owl. Endemic to Sri Lanka. Discovered only in 2004!

ABI: Maybe we will have reception. I am messaging Lakshmi, Amma.

> HIMAL *gives* ABI *his mobile phone and she turns it on.*

HIMAL: Are you telling her you got married?

ABI: I am telling her we are safe. Why would she care if I got married?

UN WORKER: No phones will work.

MADHU: What? Why?

UN WORKER: The army bombed all the satellite towers. See?

> *They all look up for a moment.*

Did you say you just got married?

HIMAL: Last night.

MADHU: Childhood sweethearts.

UN WORKER: That is excellent news! Oh I am very happy! Oh very good! No very good! Yes!

> *His delight makes them all laugh.*

I am sorry. You are not my relatives but I am very happy. Yes good.
Ninox scutulata.
MADHU: Brown Hawk Owl.
UN WORKER: Yes very good!

*

They are still walking.

UN WORKER: Biscuit?
MADHU: No thank— Yes okay. For the chicken.
UN WORKER: Shouldn't be far now.
ABI: Tell me. Why did the Germans or Swedish—
UN WORKER: Dutch, I think—
ABI: Why did they stay in Sri Lanka?
UN WORKER: There are no journalists anywhere in the Vanni. Nobody
in the rest of the world knows what is happening here. If the blond
people stay and observe, international governments will believe them.
Okay. Here we are. UN zone. No-fire zone.

> *There's smoke.*

> *He looks ahead.*

> *Moorooha ...*

> *The* UN WORKER *runs ahead.*

ABI: It's okay Amma, some smoke, I don't know what ...

> ABI *takes out her puffer.*

MADHU: Shall we go in?
HIMAL: Let's wait for the UN man to come back—

> WOMAN TWO *on a bicycle rides past.*

Friend! No-fire zone?
WOMAN TWO: Yes but no good. Army was shelling all night. Shelled
again just now, just now.
HIMAL: They bombed the no-bombing zone?
WOMAN TWO: [*exiting*] Yes!

> *They have stopped and are looking out from a rise in the road.*

> *An old* FARMER *sits nearby.*

ACT THREE

GOWRIE: Abi, tell me.

Beat.

The others look away as ABI *looks and describes.*

ABI: Many rows of white and blue tents. Cloth. Plastic. All ripped apart. Bodies. Bicycles, some trucks, all mixed up together. A child's body in a tree. No feet—

HIMAL: [*stopping her*] It's okay darling.

The UN WORKER *enters.*

UN WORKER: We asked the government to stop killing civilians, stop targeting the UN, but the government said, 'We are not targeting civilians, so there can't be any civilians killed.' Some are going back into the bunker, but I think they're going to shell us again.

MADHU: So what do we do now? Where do we go?

UN WORKER: Most staff are pulling back to PTK. Trucks are coming to take the wounded to the hospital there. But the Tigers are there too. The blonds are leaving, but I am Tamil so I cannot. This morning I would say, go with the UN. Now, I don't know.

HIMAL: PTK?

MADHU: Puthukkudiyiruppu. To the east.

ABI *shakes her puffer.*

ABI: I need more Ventolin.

MADHU: Is the hospital still there in PTK?

UN WORKER: It's the only hospital left in the war zone.

ABI: We will go to PTK. Now.

UN WORKER: Okay. Then we go east again, along A-thirty-five.

FARMER: Aiyah, Can I walk with you?

UN WORKER: Of course, brother.

*

They walk.

MADHU: [*to* GOWRIE] We are back on the highway, Amma.

ABI: Thousands of people walking. Thousands and thousands. Some just sit on the side of the road looking at the air. Dead goats, dogs. Many parts of a motorbike, as if Vayu, the God of wind, has blown it to pieces. A truck has been twisted inside out. More bodies, burned bodies, soldiers, these are just boys—

HIMAL: That's enough darling—

ABI: Look. A family. Black. Broken. Meat and cloth—

MADHU: [*stopping her saying more*] Monsoon might come soon, no?

HIMAL: But maybe the shelling will stop if it rains?

FARMER: All this used to be jungle. We used to hunt here, before the war.

MADHU: It's all bare earth now, Amma.

UN WORKER: The army travels with bulldozers. They cut it all back as they go. Trees, houses.

HIMAL: Why?

UN WORKER: So their drones can have a clear view of people.

> *They all look up.*

[*Distracting them*] So Madhu, what did you study?

MADHU: I wanted to be a veterinary surgeon.

FARMER: Very good.

UN WORKER: So?

MADHU: I lost my thumb. In a bombing.

ABI: She still studied. She finished school and came third in the region.

MADHU: And yesterday our sister in Australia graduated from her law degree.

UN WORKER: Oh very good news. Is your sister married? I have a little brother …

ABI: [*coyly*] Madhu is not married …

> *The UN WORKER is bashful. The FARMER and GOWRIE start singing a love song …*

MADHU: [*wanting to change the subject*] Uncle! What did you hunt?

FARMER: Huh?

MADHU: In the jungle. What did you hunt?

FARMER: [*in Tamil*] Lizard.

MADHU: How do you hunt lizard?

FARMER: With two hands and a sharp knife. Do deer.

MADHU: Spotted deer?

UN WORKER: Or barking deer? Or mouse deer?

FARMER: All of it.

MADHU: *Axis axis. Muntiacus muntjak. Tragalus meminna.*

FARMER: And you came third? What did the person who came first know? Everything in the universe?

ABI: [*showing* UN WORKER *the conch shell on the garland*] Do you know this one?

UN WORKER: Ah, common conch shell. No. I was never any good at molluscs.

FARMER: Nanthikkadal.

MADHU: You know this one?

FARMER: My mother is from Vattappalai next to Nanthikkadal Lagoon. Nanthikkadal. [*In Tamil*] Sea of conches. [*He points to the conch*] This one.

> MADHU *stops walking.*

MADHU: Nanthikkadal.

ABI: [*looking ahead*] There's a bus.

MADHU: Amma, Ahilan is at Nanthikkadal Lagoon. Akka!

ABI: It's stopped. The bus has stopped.

UN WORKER: [*looking at the bus*] Shit. [*To* HIMAL] We need to run.

HIMAL: What?

UN WORKER: Into the jungle. Now.

HIMAL: I'm not leaving my family.

UN WORKER: Stay here and you'll never see your family again.

ABI: Go Himal—!

UN WORKER: [*looking at the bus*] Come, come, come.

> HIMAL *looks at* ABI.

ABI: Meet us at PTK.

MADHU: No Nanthikkadal Lagoon! Thumbi is at Nanthikkadal Lagoon.

ABI: At Nanthikkadal then. Go, darling, go.

> *They start to run.*

> *A* LTTE RECRUITER, *armed with an AK47, rushes towards the group.*

RECRUITER: Stop! Get on the bus!

UN WORKER: [*showing his ID*] I'm UN! I'm UN.

RECRUITER: No more UN.

UN WORKER: What?

RECRUITER: UN on leave. Government's orders.

UN WORKER: You are LTTE, when did you start to follow government orders? You think I am on leave? On a fucking holiday? [*Holding up his pass*] I am UN. I am UN.

>*Beat.*

RECRUITER: You shouldn't be here. Go back to your compound—
UN WORKER: Come on brother—
RECRUITER: Go, go.

>*The* UN WORKER *slowly backs away.*

Go!

>*The* UN WORKER *fully turns around and walks quickly the other way, exiting.*

[*Pointing at* HIMAL] You. Come with me.
ABI: He's Singhalese!
RECRUITER: I don't care if he's Chinese—
GOWRIE: They're married.

>*Beat.*

RECRUITER: Okay. For now. [*To the* FARMER] You. Come. You will fight.
FARMER: My children already joined you.

>*Beat.*

RECRUITER: [*to* HIMAL] You married a Tamil?
HIMAL: Yes.
RECRUITER: Then you will fight for the Tamils.
HIMAL: I won't shoot! I won't shoot anyone—
RECRUITER: Can you dig?
HIMAL: What?
RECRUITER: Can you use a shovel?
HIMAL: Yes!
RECRUITER: Then you can make bunkers. Come!
ABI: No. Himal!
HIMAL: [*nodding at* ABI] Nanthikkadal. Yes?
MADHU: Himal—
HIMAL: Nanthikkadal Lagoon.

>HIMAL *exits with the* RECRUITER.

*

GOWRIE, ABI, MADHU *and the* FARMER *are walking.*

ABI: Clouds, Amma. Heavy clouds. Dark clouds. Still many people. Thousands and thousands. Madhu, look! Amma, there is a bird drinking water from a shell crater in the road.

MADHU: The curlew sandpiper. *Calidris ferruginea.* They breed in the Arctic and fly all the way to Australia. In between this one has chosen to rest and drink from this hole here in the ground in Sri Lanka.

The FARMER *sits down.*

FARMER: That sounds very good to me.

ABI stops.

ABI: It is okay Madhu, take Amma.

GOWRIE *and* MADHU *keep walking.*

[*To the* FARMER] Are you okay?

The FARMER *is barely conscious.*

FARMER: I'll just rest. Go go.

ABI: Yes?

FARMER: I'll just rest.

ABI: Yes.

She sits beside him for a moment, as if she might also stop here.

FARMER: Go on, you are not finished yet.

He gives her his water. She pays her respects to him, leaves some of her belongings there, takes the water, and runs to catch up with GOWRIE *and* MADHU.

MADHU: Is he okay?

ABI shakes her head.

ABI: Amma, a green parrot.

MADHU: Where?

ABI: There!

ABI signals that she is lying.

MADHU: Ah. Yes. *Loriculus beryllinus.* Beautiful red crown, Amma.

*

PTK hospital.

They walk through the grounds.

ABI: Puthukkudiyiruppu, Amma. PTK hospital. This is the new no-fire zone. Wounded people on the ground, on the driveway, under trees. The bags for the drips are hanging in the branches, like mangoes in the trees. Sanitary pads and saris for bandages. Wounded soldiers. Tiger boys, tiger girls.

> *An angry* DOCTOR *hurries past, talking to a* RED CROSS WORKER.
>
> *The* DOCTOR *carries a butcher's knife.*

DOCTOR: Blood bags, disinfectant, anaesthetics, especially anaesthetics. The government says we are not trained anaesthesiologists, we can only have Panadol and vitamins. We are doing amputations with a kitchen knife and they give us Panadol and vitamins.

ABI: Pardon do you have / Ventolin?

DOCTOR: There's only rice left, you can ask for water—[*gesturing 'over there'. To* RED CROSS WORKER] Butterfly clips. Gloves. Did I say gloves? Anything. Just get us anything.

> *They are gone.*

ABI: It is repeating, everything is repeating … Madhu wait with Amma, I will look for Ventolin.

> *She goes.*
>
> GOWRIE *and* MADHU *sit.*
>
> *A woman from the Tamil Rehabilitation Organisation appears.*

TRO WOMAN: Sisters. [*Offering rice*] Kanchi.

MADHU: Food! Amma, there's food.

TRO WOMAN: You can sit, sit. This is the new no-fire zone.

> ABI *returns.*

ABI: Madhu come, come with me. Hurry. Hurry! There's photos Amma. A wall covered in photos.

> *She pulls them along.*

MADHU: Akka—

ABI: Just come—

MADHU: [*to* AMMA] I'll come back, Amma.

>   ABI *points to the audience, as if to a long wall of pictures.*

ABI: Madhu? Look. You see? Is that Himal? Is that Ahilan? Can you see them?

MADHU: What is this?

ABI: The injured and the dead. Everyone who has come to this hospital. There alive. Here dead. Are they here? Can you see them?

MADHU: No—

ABI: Look! Look. Is that Himal? / No—

MADHU: Akka—

ABI: Look, just wait. There are more. / Here. Look. Look!

MADHU: Akka—

ABI: [*pulling* MADHU *away*] Shut up and look!

>   Dead. Dead. Dead. Is he here? / Can you see him?

MADHU: He is not here. Akka—

ABI: There! No. / No, it's not him.

MADHU: Abi they're not here. Listen. Himal. Ahilan. They're not here.

ABI: No?

MADHU: He is not here. You see. Their pictures are not here.

>   *A barrage of shells.*

>   *They drop to the floor.*

>   *The* DOCTOR *runs through angrily with a walkie talkie.*

DOCTOR: Can't they see the banners on the roof? Tell them to look at the banners on the roof! Listen, they are bombing us now! They are bombing the no-fire zones! Tell them wounded LTTE soldiers are not in the main building. Main building is civilians only. Hello? Hello?

>   *The walkie talkie's signal is lost.*

>   *More shelling, smoke, dust.*

*

GOWRIE, *the chicken, and the* TRO WOMAN.

MADHU *and* ABI *find her.*

MADHU: [*running towards her*] Amma!

TRO WOMAN: [*pointing her finger at them*] Do not leave your Amma!

MADHU: No, we are / very sorry.

TRO WOMAN: Do not leave her!

MADHU: Of course no.

> *Beat.*

TRO WOMAN: [*exiting*] I gave her rice. I gave you rice. But do not leave your mother!

> TRO WOMAN *leaves.*

> ABI *takes Gowrie's arm and they begin to walk again.*

ABI: Amma, come. [*They begin exiting*] They're not here, Amma. Neither of them. No Ahilan, no Himal. [*To* MADHU] Don't forget the chicken. I found Ventolin.

*

They are walking.

ABI: East. A-thirty-five. Again. Towards the sea. Mullivaikkaal. On the other side of the lagoon.

GOWRIE: Nanthikkadal.

ABI: Nanthikkadal Lagoon, Amma. There is another no-fire zone on the other side, on the beach between the lagoon and the sea.

MADHU: How many have there been now?

ABI: Three.

MADHU: How many can they have?

ABI: Any number. The war has broken open, it has its own laws.

MADHU: How long have we been walking, Akka?

ABI: Weeks? Months? A hundred years? I don't know.

MADHU: But after the beach we have nowhere else to go.

ABI: Into the sea. Under the ground. Rice paddies, Amma. Dry, no rice, no water. Still many people. Thousands and thousands and thousands …

GOWRIE: I can smell the sea.

*

Walking.

MADHU: [*suddenly realising*] I've lost my book. *Helm's Field Guide.* I don't have it anymore.

GOWRIE: It's okay, darling.

> *She repeats this.*

MADHU: Yes, doesn't matter. [*Muttering*] Brown Hawk Owl. *Ninox scutulata*. Brown Wood Owl. *Strix leptogrammica*. Chestnut-backed Owlet. *Glaucidium castanonotum*.

ABI: [*guiding* GOWRIE *around something on the ground*] Careful, kakka. We didn't come this far to step in dog shit.

GOWRIE: Abi—language!

ABI: Sorry, Amma.

> *They walk.*

> No more rice?

MADHU: Finished.

*

Walking.

ABI: I think we should kill and eat the chicken.

MADHU: No.

ABI: Somebody will.

MADHU: No.

ABI: Better it is us.

GOWRIE: No.

ABI: Okay. It was just an idea.

*

Walking.

Time passes.

ABI: One small temple tree. The flowers have just come out.

> Maybe rain over there.

> Many different kinds of cloud.

> Many different colours.

> Grey like purple, blue like grey, purple like blue, blue like elephant skin.

> Very low.

> All across the sky.

Rain.
Not here.
Not yet.
Getting too dark to see.
Time to stop?
Nice warm air.
Gentle breeze.
Keep walking?
Yes?
Yes.
Should be here soon.
Should be close.
Listen.

They listen.

The sea.
Very close.
Keep going.
Thousands and thousands.
Yes keep going.
What was that poem, Amma?

They walk into the dark and ABI *recites a poem.*

*

Morning.

ABI: Nanthikkadal, Amma.
Sea of conches.
End of the road.
Last no-fire zone.
Mullivaikkaal.
Ocean there.
Lagoon there.
In between:
Beach.
Rows and rows of white tents.
Bunkers in the ground.

Burnt lorries and buses.
Tipped over.
Thousands of people.
Tens of thousands.
Scattered all over.
Like we have been dropped from the sky.
A whole city.
Dropped from the sky on a beach.
Father James!
You see?
Full circle.
Time for fate.
Time for destiny.
[*Calling out*] Father James!

FATHER JAMES *carries sacks of milk powder.*

An ASSISTANT GOVERNMENT AGENT *is with him, also carrying sacks.*

FATHER JAMES: Ah my friends! I see you again! Abirami, come, you help me. Go with this man, help this man to carry these.

AGA MAN ONE: [*not stopping, hurrying on, to* ABI] Come, come, come.

ABI *hurries to take the bag.*

FATHER JAMES: Mrs Siva, Madhu, come with me, I'll see if we can get you some food.

ABI *hurries to follow the* AGA MAN ONE.

ABI: [*calling back*] Amma, go with Father James! I will find you!

FATHER JAMES: [*calling to her and pointing*] Come to the mango tree! I will find you there. [*To* MADHU *and* GOWRIE] I told you we would see each other again. Where is Himal?

GOWRIE: We have lost him.

FATHER JAMES: He's …?

GOWRIE: He's alive.

FATHER JAMES: Then we will find him.

GOWRIE: Father. I think Ahilan is here. Nanthikkadal.

FATHER JAMES: Your son is here?

GOWRIE: I think so.

FATHER JAMES: I will ask around, Mrs Siva. I will. You wait, I'll get you food.

*

ABI *walks with the* AGA MAN ONE, *carrying sacks.*

AGA MAN ONE: Milk powder. From Red Cross ships. [*Pointing out to sea*] You see? My job is to feed people. Last month NGOs ask me, how much food to organise? I tell them, three hundred thousand people. Government says 'arbitrary and baseless', 'wrong information'. So now I am fired but I still do my job. Now over one hundred and fifty thousand are unaccounted for. Dead, disappeared, missing? [*Shrugging*] But we still have more than one hundred thousand people on this beach. And very little food.

> *He offloads her sacks.*

ABI: What happens to everyone now?

AGA MAN ONE: Sometimes the Red Cross ships take the sick and wounded. To Trinco. Out of the war zone. Last week LTTE gave some passes to go on *Oriental Princess*. Depends if LTTE is in a good mood or bad mood.

ABI: How do you know?

AGA MAN ONE: Right now? Better to assume generally a bad mood. [*Quietly*] They are losing the war. *Oriental Princess* is coming again today. Try to get your family on. Ask a soldier to shoot you in the leg. Get out of here if you can. Government are trapping LTTE into a corner. [*Gesturing around them*] This is the corner. Everyone here is a hostage, for both sides. Stay in the corner and you will die.

*

GOWRIE, MADHU *and* FATHER JAMES.

FATHER JAMES: I have been going back and forth between the government and the LTTE to negotiate for peace. I tell the LTTE they must surrender now. I tell the government they must promise to keep the living alive. Government is coming in tighter and tighter. Best thing now is to surrender. Everybody can go in safety. I think they will do this.

ABI *runs on, excitedly.*

ABI: Amma, Madhu, hurry, come! One way out! [*Taking the chicken*] Thangacci it is time for that chicken to do some magic.

MADHU: [*resisting*] No Akka, what are you doing?

ABI: The chicken is important, but we're also important. There is one way out. Trust me, I am the bad Akka.

She takes the chicken.

*

ABI, GOWRIE, MADHU *and* FATHER JAMES.

FATHER JAMES *is negotiating with* AGA MAN TWO *from the ship.*

ABI: Amma, come! There, can you see. The Red Cross ship is not allowed to come closer than one kilometre, they send the food on small boats and then the boats will be allowed to take people back to the ship—

FATHER JAMES: He says too many. Even two is too many.

ABI: No no no!

She runs to AGA MAN TWO.

What about my mother and sister only? / Just two, just two—

AGA MAN TWO: Only one.

ABI: What?! No—

AGA MAN TWO: Only one.

ABI: No.

AGA MAN TWO: Okay, fine.

He starts to leave.

ABI: Okay.

Yes—just—

She looks at MADHU.

MADHU *wobbles her head, yes.*

Okay, yes.

AGA MAN TWO: Yes.

She runs to her mother.

ABI: Amma, just you. The Red Cross will take you, you'll be safe with them.

GOWRIE: I will not leave my daughters / and my son—

AGA MAN TWO: [*taking the chicken*] Okay yes, come come come aunty—

GOWRIE: Abi—

ABI: We will find Ahilan. Amma. We will be okay. We will stay with Father James. Yes? Father James is special, he is allowed to go both sides. We will stay with him and find Ahilan, okay—

> *Noise, shelling.*

AGA MAN TWO: No!

> AGA MAN TWO *runs through, exiting.*

ABI: No no no. What are they doing? No! The ships are going.

FATHER JAMES: The ship is turning around. / Too much shelling. Too dangerous.

ABI: No!

> AGA MAN ONE *runs on, frantic, waving at the ship.*

AGA MAN ONE: Come back! Come back! Bring the food! Where is the food?

FATHER JAMES: We need the food!

*

ABI, GOWRIE *and* MADHU.

SEWING WOMAN *sits at a sewing machine, sewing cloth into sacks.*

ABI *paces.*

Sounds of shelling.

ABI: Into the sea: not possible. Under the ground: I am not a worm. Nowhere left to go. [*To the* SEWING WOMAN] You carried a sewing machine all the way from the other side of the country?

> SEWING WOMAN *wobbles her head, yes.*

My sister carried a chicken.

> SEWING WOMAN *wobbles her head, yes.*

> FATHER JAMES *enters.*

FATHER JAMES: It is goodbye again. I am going to meet the LTTE top brass. You will see. They will surrender. It is nearly over!

ABI: [*to the* SEWING WOMAN] Why are you sewing these sandbags?

SEWING WOMAN: The Tigers ordered us to make bunkers. So we will make bunkers.

ABI: [*to* FATHER JAMES] You see? They will not surrender.

FATHER JAMES: We must always try for the best outcome first.

ABI: Nothing in this country can be decided by a human anymore. Only chaos will decide. The rule of chaos. Chaos is in charge. President Chaos and Major General Chaos and all the little chaos soldiers.

> *She smacks at a mosquito.*

Insect chaos.

GOWRIE: We have to cross the lagoon.

ABI: And go to the government side? What will they do to us? And what about Ahilan? What about Himal?

GOWRIE: Here the earth will fall on our head. Here it is only death.

> *Beat.*

ABI: Take off your blindfold and we will go.

GOWRIE: No.

MADHU: 'Any little choice I will take it.' Yes, we cross the lagoon.

GOWRIE: [*to* ABI] Mahal?

> *Beat.*

ABI: Goodbye, Father. Good luck. Good fortune. I think you are wrong, but I wish you are right.

FATHER JAMES: You will see!

> FATHER JAMES *hurries off.*

> SEWING WOMAN *stands up.*

SEWING WOMAN: Can I cross with you?

ABI: You want to try to live, huh?

> SEWING WOMAN *wobbles her head, yes.*

Okay, yes. Tonight we cross the Nanthikkadal Lagoon.

*

The revolve speeds up and becomes the Nanthikkadal.

ABI, MADHU *and* GOWRIE *are on the banks.*

The SEWING WOMAN *is with them.*

Shelling sounds.

ABI: Rain.

> The monsoon has come.

> *It begins to rain.*

> It will hide us. Come. Stay with Madhu.

> *They begin to cross,* ABI *leading.*

VOICE: [*off*] Hey!

ABI: Come come come!

> ABI *is nearly across. The others are halfway.*

> AHILAN *enters on the shore behind them, gun in hand.*

AHILAN: Turn around and come back! Nobody to leave. Come back to the shore.

ABI: [*to* GOWRIE *and* MADHU] Come!

> *The* SEWING WOMAN *crosses and exits.*

GOWRIE: Thumbi?

AHILAN: [*lifting his gun*] Return to the shore—

GOWRIE: Ahilan?

> *Beat.*

AHILAN: Amma?

> *He lowers his gun and walks into the lagoon towards them.*

MADHU: Thumbi …

> AHILAN *reaches* GOWRIE *and* MADHU *in the centre.*

> GOWRIE *touches* AHILAN'*s face.*

> *She feels his skin.*

> GOWRIE *takes* AHILAN'*s hands and puts them to her own face.*

ABI: Amma what are you doing? Madhu what is she—

MADHU: Akka it's Thumbi!

GOWRIE: Mahan. My son.

AHILAN: Amma.

> *They embrace.*

The LTTE COMMANDER *enters on the shore behind them.*

COMMANDER: Brother! What are you doing? Nobody to leave!

AHILAN: [*to his family*] You have to come back to the beach.

MADHU: They will bomb the beach. Cross the lagoon with us.

AHILAN: That man will shoot us if we cross. You must come back.

COMMANDER: What are you doing?

GOWRIE: We are not going back.

    Beat.

AHILAN: Okay Amma. You cross. I will talk to him then come.

    AHILAN *turns towards the* LTTE COMMANDER.

COMMANDER: What the hell is going on?

    MADHU *and* GOWRIE *keep crossing to the other side.*

ABI: I'm here Amma, I'm here.

AHILAN: [*to the* COMMANDER] Anna—please. This is my family.

COMMANDER: Bring them back! Nobody to leave!

AHILAN: Fifteen years.

COMMANDER: What?

AHILAN: Fifteen years I've been trying to get justice your way!

COMMANDER: Son?

AHILAN: How many more people have to die?

COMMANDER: You think if we surrender, this country will just embrace our people with open arms?

AHILAN: We're going to lose. Why are we still fighting?

COMMANDER: We win or we are nothing. Nobody to leave!

    He cocks his gun and raises it at AHILAN.

ABI: Thumbi!

    ABI *goes into the lagoon towards* AHILAN.

    ABI *reaches* AHILAN *and steps in front of him, taking his hand.*

[*To* COMMANDER] We are nobody sir! War has broken open! Out of control! But you can stop this little bit! Yes? You can stop this. Sir? Yes?

    A Sri Lankan Army SOLDIER ONE *enters on the other side.*

    He yells in Sinhala and raises his gun.

SOLDIER ONE *shoots.*

The LTTE COMMANDER *shoots.*

AHILAN *raises his gun.*

MADHU, AHILAN, SOLDIER ONE *and the* COMMANDER *die.*

The revolve continues to turn.

[*Leading* GOWRIE *around the edge of the lagoon*] I'm here Amma.
I'm here.

They walk in silence. Then:

KISHAN *enters.*

Amma …
KISHAN: Gowrie-Amma. Abi.
GOWRIE: Kishan?
KISHAN: Old friend.

Kalieaswari Srinivasan, Nadie Kammallaweera, Prakash Belawadi, Anandavalli and Rajan Velu in Belvoir St Theatre's The Jungle and the Sea, *2022 (Photo: Sriram Jeyaraman)*

ACT FOUR

The revolve continues to turn slowly.

We pick up where we left off at the end of Act Three.

GOWRIE *and* ABI *stand, wet and muddy.*

KISHAN *enters.*

He is clean and well-dressed in civilian clothes.

FATHER JAMES *waits on the side.*

ABI: Amma …
KISHAN: Gowrie-Amma. Abi.
GOWRIE: Kishan?
KISHAN: Old friend.

> KISHAN *goes to* GOWRIE, *gently takes her hand and sits her in a chair. He gives her water.*

The war is over. Here, drink. Come sit!
  The last LTTE surrendered this morning. The war is over. I am the new government agent for the north, I am here to re-establish Sri Lankan Civilian Government. You are in my compound, you are safe. Okay?
GOWRIE: Kishan. My son. My daughter.
KISHAN: Yes, I am so sorry. I have sent people to recover their bodies.
GOWRIE: We lost Himal.
KISHAN: Himal is okay.
ABI: Where is / he—
KISHAN: Abi, Himal is okay. But please listen to me. The government is putting all displaced people into camps. There is one behind this compound. Eighty thousand people in this one, fifty thousand in the next one, and so on. Once you are inside a camp it is very difficult to leave. You understand? You must go now, okay? In half an hour my car and driver will be here to take you to Colombo.
ABI: Kishan Uncle—we have to do the funeral rites for my brother and sister.
KISHAN: Yes and I have brought Father James here especially for this. Father James.

FATHER JAMES *goes to them.*

FATHER JAMES: Mrs Siva. Abi. I'm so sorry.

KISHAN: I promise you, Father James will give a proper funeral for Madhu— But you must go, leave all this with him—

ABI: And Ahilan? He's Hindu, how will we—

KISHAN: You have to leave, yes?

ABI: But what about our brother?

KISHAN: Abi. The president has ordered there must be no commemorations for any LTTE. I will do what I can, leave this with me. But you must *go*. I cannot help you after this.

LAKSHMI *enters. She is clean and well-dressed.*

ABI: Amma …

KISHAN: [*to* LAKSHMI] Ah. Come.

LAKSHMI *goes to* KISHAN.

He takes her hand and guides her to GOWRIE *and* ABI.

Gowrie-Amma, Lakshmi is here. It is Lakshmi.

GOWRIE: [*in disbelief*] Lakshmi?

LAKSHMI: Amma …

LAKSHMI *and* GOWRIE *embrace.*

KISHAN: Lakshmi has come to take you to Australia. Do you understand?

LAKSHMI: Amma. I've come to take you home. To Australia.

KISHAN: Lakshmi will take you and Abi and get you out of here. You will leave Sri Lanka. All has been organised. Okay?

LAKSHMI: Yes, Kishan Uncle, thank you—

ABI: We want to do the funeral rites for our brother as well.

KISHAN: I am the government agent but for now the army is in charge of the north. Inside this compound, you are in my trust. You get in my car to Colombo, you are in my trust. But you step outside they will put you in the camp with every other Tamil person in the area and then I cannot help you. I will do what I can, Abi.

ABI: It is not enough.

Beat.

KISHAN: [*to* GOWRIE] Gowrie-Amma, come. There is a shower, clean clothes.

GOWRIE: Abi?

ABI: It is okay, Amma.

GOWRIE: Thank you, Kishan.

KISHAN: [*to* ABI *and* LAKSHMI] My car will be here in half an hour.

> KISHAN *exits with* GOWRIE.

LAKSHMI: Abi—

> LAKSHMI *hugs* ABI.

ABI: [*looking where* KISHAN *exited*] Those motherfuckers.

LAKSHMI: Abi-Akka—

ABI: We have not come this far to eat shit and be sent away.

LAKSHMI: Abi, it's okay, / we can leave here—

ABI: Dump our brother in a mass grave in the jungle—

LAKSHMI: Everything has been organised—

ABI: Our sister given a political funeral, the good dead Tamil—

LAKSHMI: Abi-Akka we must go—

ABI: No. We must draw a line: enough.

> ABI *begins to walk out.*

LAKSHMI: Akka, where are you going?

ABI: I am going to give my brother a funeral.

> *She exits.*

> LAKSHMI *looks at* FATHER JAMES.

FATHER JAMES: It is not over.

*

Twenty minutes later. LAKSHMI *and* FATHER JAMES *are sitting.*
A Sri Lankan Army SOLDIER TWO *enters, dragging* ABI *with him.*
A local woman, DEVLA-MA, *follows them.*

SOLDIER TWO: [*calling out*] Kishan sir! Where is Kishan sir? [*To* DEVLA-MA] Move, move, you, go.

LAKSHMI: Akka—

> LAKSHMI *and* FATHER JAMES *stand.*

SOLDIER TWO: Sit down! Stay! Kishan sir! [*To* DEVLA-MA] You, go! Get out of here! Go the camp!

DEVLA-MA *stays.*

KISHAN *enters.*

KISHAN: What do you want?

KISHAN *sees* SOLDIER TWO *and* ABI.

What are you doing?

SOLDIER TWO: Kishan sir, this girl is from your compound no?

KISHAN: That girl is in my custody, yes. What is this?

SOLDIER TWO: It is treason, sir.

KISHAN: I don't understand.

SOLDIER TWO: Girl was doing funeral rites for a Tiger.

Pause.

KISHAN: [*to* SOLDIER TWO] Tell me what you saw.

SOLDIER TWO: A man came running to tell us, a girl was making a funeral in the field. We went there to see it and it was this girl, making a funeral pyre for a Tiger boy. We stopped her and one of my boys said she is the girl who was brought to you this morning, so.

KISHAN: [*to* SOLDIER TWO] Who is this woman?

SOLDIER TWO: Local woman, she came to watch the funeral. [*To* DEVLA-MA] Go to the camp!

KISHAN: [*to* DEVLA-MA] You are local?

DEVLA-MA *wobbles her head.*

Why aren't you in the camp? Why isn't she in the camp?

SOLDIER TWO: She lives in the jungle sir. Crazy woman. Probably doesn't even know there was a war.

KISHAN *looks at her.*

KISHAN: [*indicating* ABI] You were watching her? You saw what she did?

DEVLA-MA *wobbles her head.*

You stay, sit.

DEVLA-MA *sits.*

Abi. What the soldier is saying. Do you deny this?

ABI: No, of course not.

SOLDIER TWO: Treason.

LAKSHMI: Abi—

KISHAN *signals to* LAKSHMI *that he will deal with this.*

KISHAN: [*to* ABI] Tell me. Yes or no. Did you know of the law forbidding commemorations of the enemy?

ABI: Yes / of course.

LAKSHMI: Abi-Akka—

KISHAN: Did you break that law deliberately?

ABI: Kishan Uncle. It was a law made up this morning by a single man.

KISHAN: You have always been like this. Stubborn to a point.

SOLDIER TWO: [*to* KISHAN] You know this girl?

KISHAN: I have known her since she was a child, that changes nothing. [*To* ABI] The president ordered there must be no commemorations for enemies of the state.

FATHER JAMES: Kishan, you must give funeral rites to all the dead.

SOLDIER TWO *spits paan.*

KISHAN: We must draw a clear line between war and peace. Peace is a fragile, dangerous time, no? We must be clear. The LTTE is gone, and must never come back, yes? No commemoration. That is the law. [*To* ABI] Do you understand what you have done?

ABI: I prepared a funeral pyre for my brother's body.

KISHAN: Abi. You will apologise.

ABI: But Kishan Uncle, why—

LAKSHMI: Abi—

KISHAN: You will apologise publicly.

ABI: No. I will not.

KISHAN: You will apologise!

LAKSHMI: Abi-Akka—

ABI: After everything. Thirty years, my whole life—

LAKSHMI: —listen to me—

ABI: —war, violence, no freedom, no peace—

LAKSHMI: We can go.

ABI: —my father blind—

LAKSHMI: Abi.

ABI: —sister gone, brother and sister dead—

LAKSHMI: We must leave.

ABI: —after all of this now we must leave our brother rotting in the sun to be eaten by dogs? Huh? No. No more. Enough.

LAKSHMI: Stop it, they will put you in prison.

ABI: [*to* KISHAN] You want to draw a line between war and peace? Give me my brother's body to burn beside the temple.

LAKSHMI: Akka we have a chance to leave.

ABI: You go. Back to where you are from. You have my blessing. [*To* KISHAN] Give my brother's ashes to pour into the sea.

SOLDIER TWO: Army can fix this.

KISHAN: This girl is not well.

ABI: I did an ordinary thing. I prepared a funeral for my brother. I have remembered how to live.

KISHAN: Abi. Behind this house are eighty thousand people who need food, shelter, medicine. You think you matter more than all of them?

ABI: I did an ordinary thing.

KISHAN: Honour that man and you honour terrorism.

ABI: No. I honour my brother, who was still just a boy when he learnt that his government wasn't there to protect him but to hurt him. He thought he had no choice but to fight. People will not put up with living in pain.

KISHAN: The Tigers killed their own people—

ABI: They were not the first to kill.

KISHAN: Oh, we're playing that game now are we?

ABI: Death requires our reverence.

KISHAN: Your 'reverence' is for killing. For boy soldiers. For suicide bombers. For killing your own if they disagree with you.

ABI: We are born to love. We are driven to hate.

KISHAN: You are not well. You are sick.

FATHER JAMES: Even the elephants mourn their dead.

KISHAN: Elephants don't blow themselves up in crowded buses. [*To* ABI] Apologise or go to prison.

ABI: Give me my brother's body, Kishan.

LAKSHMI: For god's sake Abi—stop and think. Ahilan is *dead*. Madhu is dead. You and Amma are alive. It is a miracle! And Kishan is—for the next few minutes only, the impossible is possible. I can take you and Amma to Australia. Appa is waiting. We can be a family, we can still be a family. Just— / Shut up, shut up, shut up, and come back with me.

ABI: Lakshmi. Lakshmi. Thangaci. It is not right.

LAKSHMI: In a place like this does it matter what is right?

Beat.

ABI: Just go. You go. Kishan, let me finish what I started.

LAKSHMI: Kishan we are all that Appa has left. I cannot go back without her.

KISHAN: Like every foreigner you come here and want everything to suit you. It does not. She broke the law, she will go to prison.

LAKSHMI: Kishan Uncle, she is married to your son.

KISHAN: There is a law. According to the law she is a terrorist collaborator, she will either go to prison or the army will take her. What do you think this is? We have just been in a war!

LAKSHMI: Nobody comes out of those prisons. If the army takes her she will disappear. They will torture her—

SOLDIER TWO: Western propaganda. That does not happen.

LAKSHMI: Where is Himal? [*Calling out*] / HIMAL!

KISHAN: We are wasting time. I have work to do. [*To* SOLDIER TWO *about* ABI] You. Take her to my office, get her something to eat. She is not well. [*To* LAKSHMI] Lakshmi, please, go to my car, tell the driver to wait, stay there. Go.

SOLDIER TWO *takes* ABI *and* LAKSHMI.

FATHER JAMES: Kishan. What will you do with her?

HIMAL *enters.*

HIMAL: Thatha.

FATHER JAMES: Himal.

KISHAN: Putha. My boy. You've heard?

HIMAL: People are talking about her Thatha.

KISHAN: And what do you say?

HIMAL: Thatha. You and Amma raised me to walk the line of mindful consideration. I will not choose marriage over dharma. Rightful thinking comes first.

KISHAN: Putha. My son.

He hugs HIMAL.

We have been shaken terribly by this war. But now the war is over and it is time for peace and reconciliation. For rebuilding. This is an important moment. The course we set now will decide where we will be in ten or twenty years. A small deviation will send us a long way this way, a long way that way.

HIMAL: I agree, Thatha.

KISHAN: We must never forget the greater need. We have seen madness destroy our country. I fear anarchy more than anything. If Abi gives that boy his funeral rites, there will be anarchy. Order is the only truly good thing we can do. Everything else is arrogance. We cannot fix the world. The greater need comes first. That is the only way to peace.

FATHER JAMES: Whose need, Kishan? Whose peace?

KISHAN: What?

FATHER JAMES: You are Singhalese. The majority. Does that make your need the greater one?

KISHAN: There are no Tamil needs and Singhalese needs. No Hindu needs and Muslim needs and Buddhist needs and Christian needs. Only the same rules, for everyone. One law. And the greater need.

FATHER JAMES: Then how can we honour some of the dead, and not others?

KISHAN: Father, you and I both agree, the Tigers are gone and should never come back, no?

FATHER JAMES: Kishan. These are just sisters and brothers, daughters and sons, dragged into this and killed for fodder.

KISHAN: There is a law.

FATHER JAMES: The last LTTE surrendered this morning, yes? They raised the white flag and surrendered. And now I hear they are already dead.

KISHAN: Nothing to do with me. That is Colombo.

FATHER JAMES: Yes, exactly. You are from here, no? You are a man of the north?

KISHAN: Of course I am.

FATHER JAMES: So who is the leader of this place Kishan? You or those people in Colombo? Let us do things our own way here.

SOLDIER TWO *returns.*

Beat.

HIMAL: Thatha. The Buddha says we are a species of thinkers. We discuss together, and through that we know better. It's the most precious thing we have. I would never say to you that you are wrong. But it may be possible in this case that a different view is the right one.

KISHAN: Go on.

HIMAL: You speak of the Tigers as if they are the only ones who have been violent. As if they are the only ones guilty of terrorism. But our government—has it not been violent also? And not just to Tamil civilians, but to Singhalese civilians too? Our government has killed journalists and students. Beauty queens and politicians. Any resistance, from any part of the country, has been met with violence in return—

KISHAN: That was then. This is— What is your point?

HIMAL: You say that order is the only way to peace. But is it not possible that order can be a form of violence too? Perhaps order is just violence—done neatly. Cannot the state also conduct a form of terrorism? Does it not use violence for control? Have the people in Colombo not been doing this for many, many years now? With more resources and at a greater scale than the Tigers could ever dream of?

> *Beat.*

Thatha. Let this be the moment when we draw a line in the sand and say, both sides are to blame. And we must have the same rules for all people now. All of us must be allowed to bury our dead. To grieve those who have lost. For we have all lost. Isn't that another path to peace?

FATHER JAMES: Your son speaks with wisdom.

SOLDIER TWO: [*to* FATHER JAMES] He is not in charge.

KISHAN: I spoiled you.

HIMAL: Sorry?

KISHAN: You take everything for granted. I see that now. It is my own fault.

HIMAL: Thatha?

KISHAN: You think order is something that just magically exists? We are chaos, son. Humans are chaos. Everyone wants something. You think it is possible to just give everyone what they want? Can a family function like this? A business? A government? A country? Order is hard work. It is bloody hard work. And it is always unsatisfying. It always falls short. But what is the alternative? Your own father is trying to scratch out some sense of order in this hell that has been created for us and you, my own son, walk in here like you know everything and make it sound so easy. Everyone cannot get what they want, putha. If they do, we are done. We return to chaos.

HIMAL: Everyone says she did an ordinary thing.

KISHAN: And I do what everyone else says, huh? That is the new political leadership of the north, huh?

HIMAL: She only did what I would do for you, what you would do for me—

KISHAN: I would not give even you special treatment before the law, son.

HIMAL: You are stirring up more hatred, thatha.

KISHAN: And you are giving me stupid idealistic advice that takes no account of reality!

HIMAL: I speak for you and me and for the Gods: you go too far!

KISHAN: You have chosen to come and attack me in public?!

HIMAL: You go too far!

KISHAN: Shut up! I cannot listen to you anymore.

HIMAL: You want to talk but not to listen? / Only you can talk?

KISHAN: Oh listen, Himal speaks, / Himal speaks!

HIMAL: Only the king can talk!

KISHAN: [*to* SOLDIER TWO] Bring the woman here! Army can fix this, yes? Bring her now! Tell my driver to go, take the sister to Colombo, put her on the plane to Australia. Go! Time to clean up this mess!

> SOLDIER TWO *exits.*

HIMAL: You have lost your mind. My thatha has lost his mind.

FATHER JAMES: Kishan, what will you do with her?

KISHAN: I WILL SOLVE THE PROBLEM SHE HAS CAUSED!

FATHER JAMES: Yes sir. But what will you do with her?

> KISHAN *ignores* FATHER JAMES.

> SOLDIER TWO *returns with* ABI.

> HIMAL *goes to her.*

HIMAL: Abi.

> *They touch.*

> *But then* ABI *turns to* KISHAN.

ABI: Kishan-uncle. Give me my brother's body. Let me finish what I've started.

> KISHAN *ignores them.*

SOLDIER TWO: Sir? Army will fix this, no?

FATHER JAMES: Kishan, they will kill her.

ABI: If one death was enough then kill me twice. A hundred times. I will take all their deaths. If that will bring this to an end. But it will not. This will not. [*To* KISHAN] You will not. Give me my brother.

SOLDIER TWO: People will talk about this woman, sir.

ABI: Give me Ahilan.

KISHAN: Away from the River Per, up a small mountain deep in the jungle, there is an old temple where only the Baya birds and the spotted deer still go. That will be her prison.

SOLDIER TWO: Sir, that is not a real prison—

KISHAN: I declare it is.

HIMAL: Thatha, let her go!

SOLDIER TWO: She is a traitor!

KISHAN: I am the government agent. This is a political matter.

FATHER JAMES: Kishan, if the army knows where she will be, they will kill her—

ABI: Thousands and thousands and / thousands and thousands—

SOLDIER TWO: This is ridiculous!

HIMAL: Thatha. You can stop this. Let her go.

KISHAN: I have done everything I can.

ABI: —thousands and thousands and thousands. Alive and dead at the same time.

She is no longer able to stand. She sits on the ground.

FATHER JAMES *sits with her.*

Almost all of us did not want this to happen. And yet we let it happen. Why and how?

FATHER JAMES: I don't know.

ABI: We found Ahilan on the banks of the Nanthikkadal Lagoon, just in time for his death. Chaos or destiny, Father?

FATHER JAMES: No. That was not chaos. That was not destiny. That horror was done to all of us on purpose. For power. For control.

HIMAL: [*whispering*] Abi, apologise.

ABI: I am already dead. Look.

She looks at the audience.

I see the living. Many people. Who will speak for me?

KISHAN: No-one will speak for you.

SOLDIER TWO *stands.*

ABI: Who will speak for us?

KISHAN: You see. Nobody.

HIMAL: [*whispering*] Apologise.

ABI: Honour my sister and disgrace my brother and we will always be
   dead. Give me my brother's ashes to pour into the sea, and life will
   begin again. Give us all our brothers and sisters.

KISHAN: [*to* SOLDIER TWO] You. Take her to the temple now.

SOLDIER TWO: The army should fix this.

ABI: Give us all our dead.

KISHAN: Do it! Now!

DEVLA-MA *stands.*

DEVLA-MA: Think carefully, Kishan. You are on the edge of a cliff.

They turn to her.

KISHAN: What are you talking about?

DEVLA-MA: This morning I took my usual seat
   Beneath the boabab tree
   To listen to the curlew sandpipers
   In the deep branches,
   But even as I took my seat I heard
   A screaming frenzy
   And I knew at once
   The curlews were tearing themselves apart in the sky.
   I made an offering to the forest goddess
   Dark-blue Valli
   But the fire
   Wouldn't light.
   I laid three coconuts and cracked them,
   White flesh was grey,
   Putrid smell.
   All this screaming frenzy,
   Stench,
   Silent Gods,
   The broken language of the earth,
   The cause of this is you
   Kishan.

Come here, child. Stop and think. It is normal in crazy times to do stupid things. But if a man takes a wrong turn, he goes back and finds his way, it's all okay child. So don't stab the dead. Wash your face, clear your head, step back, think again. I have your good at heart, Kishan. My words are good. And it is good to learn from good words. Stop and think. Think again.

Beat.

KISHAN: Am I the last sane person in Sri Lanka?

DEVLA-MA: You are the least sane.

KISHAN: I'm not going to trade insults with someone who makes offerings to a forest.

DEVLA-MA: You already have.

KISHAN: With respect. You talk to birds.

DEVLA-MA: Don't provoke me Kishan.

KISHAN: Crazy lady, you have been alone in the jungle too long.

DEVLA-MA: Before the sun flies across the sky once more
You will exchange
Corpse for corpse
From your own living blood
For what you left
On the battlefield,
For burying
One child
And refusing funeral
To another dead.
It was not for you to decide.
For this there lies in wait for you
The fate of all stupidity
That smashes
Stubborn men
And you will be caught
In justice
Just as full of pain
To you
As yours
To those

Brother dead
And living sister
You have wronged.
Not long now before
The cries and wails
Of pain and grief
Across the north
Will rise in your house
And broken bodies
Blood
Bones
Dead faces
Will populate the fields
Of your mind
Night and day
For the long
Time
To come.
These words are arrows.
I am the archer.
You are the target,
Provocative Kishan.
They are aimed
At your heart
And they strike
Deep
And hurt.

[*Exiting*] 'The war is over.' Huh. The war will not be over in this country until long after all the living are dead …

She is gone.

KISHAN *is silent.*

ABI *walks to a conch lying on the floor.*

FATHER JAMES: [*to* KISHAN] That venerable woman has never been wrong.
SOLDIER TWO: [*to* KISHAN] Sir—
FATHER JAMES: She has never been wrong—
SOLDIER TWO: Think carefully, sir—

FATHER JAMES: Release the girl. / Give her brother a funeral.

SOLDIER TWO: You. Shut up!

KISHAN: It is too late.

HIMAL: It is not too late, thatha. / It is your choice.

SOLDIER TWO: SIT DOWN. SHUT UP.

FATHER JAMES: It is right, Kishan. / It is the right thing.

> ABI *blows the conch.*

SOLDIER TWO: [*calling out in Sinhala*] Soldiers! I need back up! Soldiers, come here now. Right now!

> SOLDIER TWO *runs off.*

> GOWRIE *enters. She has heard the conch. She holds a bell.*

KISHAN: [*to* FATHER JAMES] Tell me what to do.

FATHER JAMES: Let her go man! Give the boy a funeral!

HIMAL: Let her go, thatha.

KISHAN: [*to* FATHER JAMES] Yes?

FATHER JAMES: Yes! Go! Do it with your own hands! Go!

> *Beat.*

KISHAN: [*to* ABI] Yes. Abi, give the boy his funeral.

ABI: Yes?

KISHAN: Yes.

> ABI *rings the bell and walks, calling out a funeral prayer.*

> GOWRIE *joins in the prayer.*

> HIMAL, KISHAN *and* FATHER JAMES *follow her.*

> SOLDIER TWO *re-enters and raises his gun.*

> FATHER JAMES, HIMAL *and* ABI—*in that order—are killed by* SOLDIER TWO.

> KISHAN *falls to his knees.*

SOLDIER TWO: [*in Sinhala, to* KISHAN] This man is under arrest, he broke the law, [*in Sinhala and English*] commemorations of the enemy are not allowed. Time to clean up! [*In English*] No more war. Only peace! Only peace! Only peace!

> SOLDIER TWO *drags* KISHAN *off.*

ACT FIVE

Sydney 2022.

LAKSHMI *is on the phone, listening.*

SIVA *(blind), confident that* LAKSHMI *is not looking, pours a spoonful of sugar into his tea; then another, then another, then another.*

LAKSHMI *turns to* SIVA.

LAKSHMI: Appa. They have found the bodies.

> *Pause.*

> SIVA *wobbles his head.*

We're coming, Amma. We're coming as soon as we can, okay?

> LAKSHMI *hangs up the phone.*

> SIVA *stands.*

SIVA: We are going to the tea house next to the mosque.

> *He begins to exit.*

LAKSHMI: What? Where? Appa!
SIVA: Rahma Mosque, Railway Street, Guildford.

*

Rahma Mosque.

SALIM *enters.*

SALIM: Siva.
SIVA: Salim, I heard that you moved to Australia and you worked here now. We live down the road, you know.
SALIM: Is that so.

> *Pause.*

SIVA: Salim they have found the bodies of our children. My daughter Lakshmi must go to Sri Lanka. They won't let me on a plane, I'm not well, I'm going to die soon. Can I stay with you?

> SALIM *considers.*

SALIM: Okay.

> SIVA *turns to his daughter.*

SIVA: Go child. You've packed your bags. Go.
SALIM: Go, Lakshmi. I'll take care of him.
SIVA: I'll see you when you're back, Lakshmi.

> LAKSHMI *hugs her father and leaves.*

SALIM: Why are you really here?
SIVA: Salim, forgive me.

> *Beat.*

SALIM: Siva … Sit. Wait.

> SALIM *leaves* SIVA.

> SIVA *sits and waits.*

Prakash Belawadi, Jacob Rajan and Rajan Velu in Belvoir St Theatre's The Jungle and the Sea, *2022 (Photo: Sriram Jeyaraman)*

*

Nanthikkadal, 2022.

LAKSHMI *and* GOWRIE.

GOWRIE *holds the conch shell from Act Four.*

LAKSHMI: Amma, Nanthikkadal.
GOWRIE: The last place I held my son.

> *Beat.*

What will happen now?
LAKSHMI: Kishan has been working with an NGO to identify the bones. Four volunteers, from the temples and the church, picked up the remains from the site this morning. They're driving them here. They'll hand them over to us. We can give them the proper rites.
GOWRIE: How did they find them?

> KISHAN *enters.*

LAKSHMI: The Sri Lankan Government are putting a new resort here. The builders were putting in the foundations when they uncovered a mass grave.
KISHAN: Gowrie-Amma. Lakshmi. The volunteers have collected the remains. They are waiting in the car.

> GOWRIE *wobbles her head.*

GOWRIE: Kishan come. Lakshmi. Come.

> KISHAN *and* LAKSHMI *gather around* GOWRIE.

> *She puts their hands on the conch.*

In memory of all who have died, and have disappeared. [*In Tamil*] We will never forget.
KISHAN: [*in Sinhala*] We will never forget.
LAKSHMI: We will never forget.
GOWRIE: [*to* LAKSHMI] Go on, child.

> *Beat.*

LAKSHMI: [*to* KISHAN] When I was a kid I used to call you 'Kishan-my-future-uncle-in-law.'
KISHAN: I remember.

LAKSHMI: What changed, uncle?

KISHAN: We went down different paths.

>*Beat.*

LAKSHMI: Kishan. I'm helping with a case. About the end of the war. The missing. There are other cases too, about Navali, the bombing of our church. We need names, testimony, witnesses, evidence.

KISHAN: A case? A legal case?

LAKSHMI: Yes.

KISHAN: For what purpose, Lakshmi?

LAKSHMI: To say publicly what happened to us, and who was responsible.

KISHAN: And then?

LAKSHMI: The UN says seventy thousand people went missing during the war. Now, after a decade of silence, the former president has said that they are all dead. And you don't have any questions?

KISHAN: How will we ever have peace if we don't leave the past behind?

LAKSHMI: To leave the past behind we must first tell the truth of what happened.

KISHAN: There are so many truths.

LAKSHMI: Then we will tell them all.

*

SALIM *returns and sits next to* SIVA.

SIVA: Salim. Forgive me.

SALIM: Siva. I'm not the one you need forgiveness from.

>*Beat.*

Stay as long as you need.

>SALIM *goes.*

>SIVA *closes his eyes.*

*

KISHAN: Lakshmi, I can't—

LAKSHMI: Kishan, we are all mixed up in this. I gave money to the Tigers. Multiple times.

>GOWRIE *turns to her daughter.*

Appa doesn't know. After what happened I was angry. I felt powerless.

Beat.

KISHAN: That day, July 1995, when they bombed the church, Siva asked me to check with my superiors about places of worship being safe—

LAKSHMI: I remember.

KISHAN: They told me of course. But deep down I knew. I knew they could be lying.

Beat.

I did nothing. Each time they went after the Tamils, I did nothing. Until eventually, they came after us too.

Beat.

LAKSHMI: So. Will you do it?

KISHAN: I could be punished.

LAKSHMI: So could I.

Beat.

KISHAN: Okay. For my son. For your sisters. For your brother. Yes. I will do it. I will help you with the case.

LAKSHMI: Okay. Good. That is good. Amma, that's good.

GOWRIE: Okay, Kishan.

KISHAN *motions to the volunteers offstage to enter.*

The actors playing ABI, AHILAN, MADHU *and* HIMAL *enter.*

LAKSHMI: Amma. They're here. Your children are here.

GOWRIE: They are together again?

LAKSHMI: Yes, Amma. We're all here.

Pause.

GOWRIE *takes off her blindfold.*

The revolve stops.

GOWRIE *adjusts to the light.*

She looks at the dead.

She looks at KISHAN.

She looks at LAKSHMI.

She touches Lakshmi's face.

GOWRIE: Kunju, at the end of the great stories, the old ones go into the jungle to find peace. The young ones stay behind to live.

Beat.

I know you're an atheist. But I can tell you, kunju, that pain is a God. Love is a God. Death is a God. And they smash the proud, again and again, until at last, we become wise.

LAKSHMI: Love bears all things.

GOWRIE: [*nodding*] Go my child.

LAKSHMI *and* KISHAN *leave.*

GOWRIE *dances for her family, and then sits down with them, to rest.*

THE END

Prakash Belawadi and Emma Harvie in Belvoir St Theatre's The Jungle and the Sea, *2022 (Photo: Sriram Jeyaraman)*

www.currency.com.au

Visit Currency Press' website now to:

- Buy your books online
- Browse through our full list of titles, from plays to screenplays, books on theatre, film and music, and more
- Choose a play for your school or amateur performance group by cast size and gender
- Obtain information about performance rights
- Find out about theatre productions and other performing arts news across Australia
- For students, read our study guides
- For teachers, access syllabus and other relevant information
- Sign up for our email newsletter

The performing arts publisher

www.ingramcontent.com/pod-product-compliance
Lightning Source LLC
Chambersburg PA
CBHW050017090426
42734CB00021B/3309